Foreword by
Tim Gurrister, Journalist

She Knew No Fear

The True Story of Pioneer Jane McKetchnie Walton's
Incredible Journey and Untimely Death

Jane M. Walton

Written by Michael R. King

(Revised Edition of *Jane... A Woman's Determination and the Wild-West Frontier*)

Published 2021 by Profiling Evil, LLC

She Knew No Fear: The True Story of Pioneer Jane McKetchnie Walton's Incredible Journey and Untimely Death

©2021 by Profiling Evil, LLC and Mike King All rights reserved. Printed in the United States of America. No part of this book may be used or reproduced in any manner whatsoever without the express written permission of the author and the owner of these rights.

For permission contact the publisher at:
Profiling Evil, LLC • ProfilingEvil@gmail.com
ProfilingEvil.com

Cover design by Circa3, Tyler Cahoon, Whitney Cahoon and Scott Wiser.

ISBN (Hardback): 978-1-7362374-5-8
ISBN (Paperback): 978-1-7362374-6-5
ISBN (eBook): 978-1-7362374-7-2
ISBN (Audio): 978-1-7362374-8-9

Awake remembrance of these valiant dead
　　And with your puissant arm renew their feats:
You are their heir; you sit upon their throne;
　　The blood and courage that renowned them
Runs in your veins;
　　　　　　　　　　　- Henry V, William Shakespeare

Foreword
by Tim Gurrister

Let me introduce... Jane. I first met Jane sitting down to a lunch with her great-great-grandson Mike King. He wanted to write a book. She was coyly layered in his stack of family journals, letters, diaries and other historical documents, a collection he'd been gathering all his adult life. Until that day the achievement of American pioneers was a stereotype, their "privations, trials and tribulations" just clichés we overfed, air-conditioned, pampered progeny today give little thought to.

Life from the 1860s to the turn of the century doesn't focus until you read it from the accounts left by those who lived through those decades, hoping for a shot at walking the American plains, if the sharks don't get you! The Atlantic crossing from the Old World came aboard wooden steamships crowded with hardy souls peering at each other, wondering who they would be burying at sea.

Mike's Jane had lost her father to typhoid and her grandfather to a stroke when she took her Atlantic leap at age four. By age six, she'd seen more death firsthand than the rest of us glimpse in a lifetime—on the plains buried in shallow graves that were quickly left behind.

Whatever your religious beliefs, spiritual metabolism, nod to a higher power, to my mind it's logical, intellectual, to wonder if there is a settlement of the American frontier without faith. It seems pulling at something so monumental couldn't even be attempted if those taking the gamble didn't subscribe to some idea of a cosmic method behind it all, some sense that they weren't alone. Likely the West would not have been won without faith.

Thank you Jane. And thanks Mike for those childhood years in smaller pants paying attention to all the family stories.

Author's Note

Throughout my life I had heard tales of my great-great-grandmother, Jane McKechnie Walton, and her incredible journeys across the Atlantic Ocean and up the Mississippi River. How, as a seven-year-old girl in 1852, she had walked across the American plains to her destination in the Utah Territory. Jane would eventually marry and with her husband, Charles, would settle into a life of simplicity on a peaceful homestead in a remote part of northern Utah. Unfortunately, life for Jane was not meant to be simple or peaceful. Jane and Charles would soon be asked by their church to take their young family to the four corners area of Utah to help establish new settlements. Always faithful and obedient, the two would accept the assignment and unknowingly become part of the most harrowing episode in Utah pioneer history—conquering the infamous Hole in the Rock.

After nearly 40 years of investigative work, my natural inclinations led me to research the nearly unbelievable tales that had been handed down through the generations. Along with the many stories, there were questions surrounding Jane's untimely death, and I felt compelled to put some investigative experience to use. The circumstances leading up to my discoveries would be remarkable, and to this day unexplainable.

CONTENTS

Chapter One
Beginnings 1

Chapter Two
Farewell 19

Chapter Three
Seafarer 33

Chapter Four
The Mighty Mississippi 43

Chapter Five
One Thousand, One Hundred Miles 57

Chapter Six
Day After Day They Walked 65

Chapter Seven
The Great Salt Lake Valley 81

Chapter Eight
Jane and Charles 101

Chapter Nine
A Warrior is Born 115

Chapter Ten
Plenty of "Stickie-ta-gudy" 151

Chapter Eleven
"Fire in the Hole" 165

CONTENTS

Chapter Twelve
Bluff 177

Chapter Thirteen
Posey 191

Chapter Fourteen
"Me Want Biscuit!" 197

Chapter Fifteen
A Snowy Solar Eclipse 209

Chapter Sixteen
Ruffian 219

Chapter Seventeen
A Fateful Night 225

Chapter Eighteen
The Investigation 237

Chapter Nineteen
Afterword 245

Acknowledgements 257

Chapter Notes 261

Bibliography 265

Chapter One
Beginnings

A light fog hung over the valley the morning of July 24, 1891, nudging memories of pioneer Jane McKechnie Walton's ancestral Scotland. She paused on the porch of her handcrafted cabin at the base of Monticello Utah's Blue Mountains as her hazel eyes scanned the terrain that she had made her own. Although it was well into July, there was enough of a chill to mist the air and provoke her to drop a shawl over her shoulders. As she ambled to the well for a bucket of water, Jane could see her husband, Charles, silhouetted against the walls of their dimly lit barn, tending to the animals. Her thoughts turned to memories of the life she and Charles had endured together.

Jane reflected on her younger years before she met Charles. When she was very young, her family had chosen to leave their beautiful Scottish homeland and travel to the desert mountains of Utah. Along the way, Jane had braved hurricanes and witnessed burials at sea. She had traveled the Mississippi River and walked the American plains.

Now, more than 40 years and 10,000 miles had led Jane and Charles to these serene times. Unbeknownst to them, these many years were winding down to this one day. As she pumped the well water into her tin bucket, Jane paused to breathe in the fresh, clean, country air. She was never one to complain about her rugged existence on the frontier, nor wish for a softer, less savaged lifestyle. Jane had been born across the sea in a rain-soaked land of perpetual cloudiness. Throughout the years, she had taken care to shield her fair Scottish complexion from the harsh sun of her high-mountain desert home. Her face was not a testament to the brutal circumstances she had endured. However, her once auburn colored hair was now peppered with silver.

The rolling hills of her native Scotland were a distant memory and Jane had grown to love her home in the desert. She paused to watch the earliest rays of sunlight touch the top of the Blue Mountain Range. Then slowly, but with reliable determination, the splashes and stripes of sunshine stretched across the cathedral of mountains and onto the awestruck valley below. This was Jane's favorite time of day. The chimney stacks and roof-topped skylines of Edinburgh had long since given way to the beauty of frontier horizons.

* * * * * *

Jane McKechnie Walton's life began much differently than it ended. She was born in Edinburgh, Scotland on July 16, 1846, and was the second daughter to John McKechnie and Jean Tinto Bee McKechnie (aka Jane Tinto Bee). She had one older sister, Georgina, who had been born a year earlier on April 5th. Both of

Jane's parents were devout Presbyterians who were married two years earlier on July 12, 1844, in the Saint Cuthbert's Parish Church in Edinburgh. They began their married life together in a small row house at 57 Bristol Street. By the time Jane was born, the family had moved to the harbor area of Edinburgh in a neighboring community called Leith.

Jane's father, John, was a skilled brass-founder and bell-molder by trade and was considered a very good craftsman by those in his community. As with most people of the time, finding enough work was a difficult task and when John was out of work, the family was in financial turmoil. When he was able to work, however, John made a good living and provided a comfortable life for his growing family. His attention to detail and his tireless work ethic mirrored his own father's and seemed almost genetic. John hoped that his own children would someday share in his determination and perseverance.

A bell was central to every community in Scotland, serving much like a shared heartbeat. The reverberating chime announced to city residents the beginning and end of each day, and when to worship, work, and play. The process for casting bells during the 1840s relied on long-tested, generational skills. John had been taught the craft of bell molding by his father. It was a trade that had been handed down from father to son for nearly 600 years.

Most young men of the era learned to work at a very young age and the opportunity to choose a profession or to ponder various career paths was usually not an option. For many young men, the occupation of the father governed the line of business followed by the son. John, no doubt, had visions of exciting professions such as serving as a soldier in the army, or as a constable in Edinburgh. But as the years rolled by, he was given more and more responsibility in his father's trade and eventually he, too, became a bell molder.

No mistake should be made, however; a bell molder was a career worthy of distinction.

Molding bells was not a position that could be filled by just anyone. A bell-molder needed to possess a high degree of personal integrity along with a resolute work ethic. A blemish in a bell could often be ground away and covered up, but if the imperfection happened to be in a critical place, the quality of sound or the physical integrity of the bell could suffer. John had no one looking over his shoulder or inspecting his work, so everything hinged on his personal integrity that wouldn't allow shoddy work to be a part of any bell he built. John was often selected to build a bell based solely on his reputation for quality work, with price being a secondary consideration.

Regardless of a bell's size, the method for molding it was much the same—it had to be crafted in a manner that ensured both strength and quality of sound. John learned at an early age that the creation of the core of the bell was the most important step in ensuring the bell's integrity and he often remarked that a properly constructed mold of sand and brick was the fundamental key to success.

The bell's form had to be perfectly rounded, shaped, and hardened—able to withstand tremendous heat and the rigors of the intense refining process that differentiated bells built by John's family and other bells of lesser quality. John would painstakingly pile sand over the bricks and then skillfully heat and cure the emerging mound. Like a master chef, he knew when to add a little more heat to the fire or a dash more sand. Then, with more sand and bricks and additional heating and curing, he would finish the interior of the bell.

Once the core was firm, John would laboriously paint a compound over it to create a false bell. Molten ore would then be poured to cover the false bell where a housing would be constructed over the entire structure. This delicate process of building up the bell housing was completed by setting an iron casing over the clay until it would collapse under heat at the appointed time. John would then pour the molten bronze throughout the housing mold at a temperature of over two thousand degrees to finalize his creation. Once completed, he would bury the bell in the ground for as much as two weeks at a time in order to properly cool and cure it. Afterward, he would carefully examine, grind, touchup, and polish the bell in preparation for its public début. Though an intricate, slow, and often tedious process, the completed bell would become the beacon of a community and the bell's creator would be spoken of with respect for generations to come.

John's creation of one particular bell in the early 1840s required exceptional care and tedious craftsmanship because the bell was destined to ring in the St. Cuthbert's Parrish Church near his home in Edinburgh. As a member of the church, John would hear the bell's tone, firsthand, each week as he attended church services. When he began building the bell in 1840, he was unaware of its special destiny. Four years later it would ring in celebration at his own wedding ceremony. John and Jean were married in the church shortly after the bell was finished.

Plying his trade and building a monument to his own craftsmanship made for long hours of painstaking attention to detail. John wanted his work to be perfect not only because he lived and worked in the area where his bells hung, but he also needed to keep the family business running, and thus the family's reputation. Consequently, many late nights were spent working by the light of oil-burning lamps, often with his wife, Jean, by his side.

John McKechnie continued to construct bells in Edinburgh for several years during which time the two little girls, Georgina and Jane, were born to the couple. While two beautiful, healthy little girls were more than many families could ask for, John hoped for a son to carry on the family name and learn the skills of the bell molder. When Jean discovered she was pregnant for a third time she excitedly shared the news with John and together they hoped their new baby might be their long-awaited son.

As John and Jean awaited the arrival of their new baby, John began to suffer what he assumed were merely work-related symptoms from stress and fatigue. At first, he was able to ignore the headaches, weakness and stomach pain, and continued working. Within a few weeks, he had lost his appetite and developed rose-colored rashes on his body. Being an experienced bell-molder, John was used to the headaches and rashes that accompanied his daily dealings with molten steel, but when these small ailments began to evolve into weight loss and high fevers, he and Jean grew concerned. Jean suggested that he see a doctor, but John brushed the notion aside feeling it would be too expensive. Surely, he thought, this would pass. For a while, it did.

After a month of dealing with his symptoms and seeing a dramatic increase in sickness and death throughout the city of Edinburgh, John worried that he might be suffering from the same disease. Could it be typhoid? The very thought of it was too horrible to consider. He began to miss many days of work and bells went unfinished. Customers became frustrated with the delays, which in turn increased John's anxiety. He and Jean discussed the idea of moving from the city to the country, in hopes the fresh air would cure his ailments and ease his suffering. Almost immediately the couple began looking for suitable living quarters away from Edinburgh.

The trips to the country and the search for a home away from the city always made John feel better. After a weekend in the countryside, his strength would somewhat return and he was able to work longer hours, but it was only a temporary reprieve. Within a few days, the ailments would return, and his fatigue would be so great that he couldn't complete a full workday. He blamed his lack of energy and lethargy on pollution in Edinburgh and often remarked that the open air of the countryside rejuvenated him. Unfortunately, as time passed, even trips to the country didn't seem to help.

Typhoid fever was racing throughout the British Isles, claiming thousands of lives. The original source of the epidemic disease was closely linked to bad sanitation habits and the cramped living conditions of the poorer neighborhoods and now, fear ran rampant throughout all of Edinburgh and its bordering communities. Many people wondered if the disease was instantly contagious and spread by merely touching those who were contaminated. Others, relying only on old tales of previous generations, wondered if the plague was caused by unhealthy vapors in the air.

The family's worst fear was confirmed as John's health declined and he became gravely ill. John McKechnie joined the ranks of the dead on January 3, 1848. He never had the chance to see his long-awaited heir, a son, born April 20th of that same year. Fittingly, Jean named the baby after her departed husband.

Jean wasn't alone in her mourning. Her mother, Janet, had lost her husband, George Bee, five years earlier. Janet's experience with bereavement was consoling to her daughter as mother and daughter turned to each other for comfort. Janet had learned how to handle her personal finances after the loss of George and now found herself teaching Jean how to do the same. Gratefully, George Bee was a wise money manager and he had taught Janet during their marriage how to handle financial matters. George had been self-sufficient and was a well-known person of influence.

The Bee family had been farmers throughout the generations. They lived in conditions considered far better than most of that era. Although Jean's father had been afflicted with palsy (possibly a stroke) a few years before his death, from which he lost the entire use of one side of his body and the ability to speak, the family enjoyed a good life. Prior to his decline in health and eventual death, George Bee was a builder and a "Burgess." Burgesses were craftsmen and merchants who also owned property in the burghs. As a Burgess, he was allowed to do business without paying taxes or fees—a privilege that was obtained either through marriage, by purchasing the liberties outright or through blood-inheritance. The Bees were tradesmen and titled landowners, yet they faced financial burdens and the changing national financial conditions caused them to lose most of their assets.

When Jean's father George, and mother, Janet, were starting their life together, the city of Edinburgh was facing financial turmoil from mismanagement and corruption in the government, particularly at the parliamentary level. Edinburgh was experiencing a growing pollution from industry and the city's water supply and sewer system were failing. Out of necessity, a localized assembly was set up to run the affairs of the city. This new governing body of commissioners was elected by the home and property owners in the area and soon, the commissioners inherited the responsibility of running the city. This change in government abolished some of the benefits the Burgesses had previously enjoyed, although the title continued to be used to describe their standing in the community. The laws of the day made Jean and her sister, Joanna's, younger brother Richard heir to their father's estate.

Janet took Jean into her home after John's death and together they shared a rare bond after laying the patriarchs to rest. Janet was also able to help her young daughter find work. It was nearly eighteen months after John's death before Jean could begin to notice brighter days. Her growing children were healthy, and she was able to find work caring for two rich, elderly women in the Edinburgh city center—it was all she could ask for and more.

One day, while walking to the home of the two spinsters she was caring for, Jean met two young men. The pair were church missionaries who were amiable enough, but when they invited Jean to learn about their religion, she bid them farewell. Throughout the day however, Jean could not rid her thoughts of the two young missionaries. Once her work day was over, she decided to seek them out.

When she met the two young men again, she was inspired by the words of one of them—an American named Robert Gault. He told her of a restored gospel of Jesus Christ led by a living prophet named Joseph Smith. Gault spoke of Smith's revelations, and his visions of God and Jesus Christ, and other celestial beings. He explained that Smith had been told in these visitations that no existing church currently taught and administered the gospel as it was done when Jesus Christ was personally on the earth. This was a powerful message to Jean and supported her frustration with what she considered to be the rather static teachings imparted for centuries by mainstream churches, both Catholic and Protestant.

One evening while Jean listened to the missionaries teach her from the scriptures, they spoke of a principal called, "eternal life"— a continuation of life beyond the grave, and that she could be reunited with her husband again. They shared scriptures with Jean from both the Bible and another text of scriptures called the Book of Mormon. The missionaries testified that those who died were not forever gone, but they had returned home to the God who created them. As the discussion continued, the missionaries told Jane that her relationship with John was not destined to end at his death, but could continue forever—they could "seal" or bind their children to them throughout the eternities. With the pain of John's death still aching in her heart, this message brought her hope. Convinced of the truthfulness of their message, Jean knew that she wanted to become a member of this new church.

Jean kept her spiritual conversion a secret while she continued to meet with the missionaries. In time she announced to her mother and family her intentions to join this church. The announcement did not go over as well as she had hoped. Jean's mother was very concerned and begged her daughter to reconsider, or at least meet with the family's minister to discuss it further. After a great deal of persuasion from her mother and brother Richard, Jean agreed. She actually looked forward to speaking with the minister; she had just as many questions for him as she figured he would have for her. Naively, she thought he would be impressed with her newfound knowledge and would support her decision.

When the day came to meet with the minister, Jean strode up the steps to the church she had attended as a child and boldly pushed the tall wooden doors open. The minister politely invited her into his modest office and thanked her for coming to visit him. The cleric had served the Bee family for years and they had always followed his guidance. Once in the minister's presence, Jean shared her conversion story and boldly bore witness of her new relationship with Jesus Christ and her desire to be baptized into the Church of Jesus Christ of Latter-day Saints as soon as possible. She thought he would respect her search for truth and perhaps ask her how their historic Presbyterianism had failed her.

The minister listened quietly, without interjection or response. After sharing her story with conviction, Jean asked the minister if she could set up a meeting between the missionaries and the minister himself, so that he could personally talk with them. She was startled at how quickly her long-time minister refused any consideration. He simply said, "I'll have nothing to do with them." The minister told Jean that he was disappointed in her for wanting to join the new faith and said her soul was in jeopardy if she continued down the poorly chosen path. As she reiterated her belief in what she had heard, he only became more forceful and demanding. With that, she left his office.

When Jean returned home from the church, she did not share any of the details of the discussion with her mother. She busied herself with the care of her three children. Later that night, almost skulking in the dark and drizzle, the minister came to Janet and Jean's home to discuss the earlier events of the evening. Janet was surprised the minister would take the time to personally come to her home, given the late hour and the stormy weather outside. Honored at his presence, she invited him in and offered him a cup of tea. As he entered the house, he asked Janet if he could speak to her privately.

Over the course of the next hour and a half, the minister spoke bluntly to Janet about Jean's impending spiritual damnation and the earthly consequence if she left the Presbyterian fold for the "Mormons". He told her that Jean was certainly walking the spiritual plank, likely taking her children with her into the shoals of sin and the dark waters of depredation, his metaphors drowning each other.

With relentless warnings, the minister built enough fear and trepidation into Janet's heart concerning her daughter that he convinced her a "tough love" approach was the only way they could possibly save Jean's soul. With that, Jean was summoned to the kitchen where she was given the ultimatum to forsake her beliefs or face immediate expulsion from the family home. Jean was speechless as she stared at her mother, but Janet firmly repeated the words to her, stating that she would have to take her children and leave Janet's home forever if she continued in her quest to join the Latter-day Saint faith. All the while the suddenly silent minister nodded his head in support while standing behind Jean.

Janet turned toward the window. It was dark and dreary outside. The minister moved closer to her and placed his hand on her shoulder in support of the stance she had taken. Jean suddenly felt a surge of pain well up inside of her. Fighting back tears, she walked out of the kitchen. The damp wind blew Jean's hair back as she opened the door of the house and looked into the gloomy night. She gathered her three stunned children together with the few belongings they could carry, and the four of them stepped from Janet's home into the drizzle of the Scottish night. Janet watched stoically as her daughter, with her grandchildren in tow, faded into the night. As Jean looked over her shoulder at her mother's house, the image of Janet and the minister sadly waving goodbye became imprinted in her memory forever.

Not knowing where to turn, Jean decided to go to the missionaries to appeal for help. They kindly took her and her children in and made them comfortable for the night. By midday next, the church Jean would soon join had helped her secure lodging until she could find a place to live. With the help of the missionaries, she was able to get additional work in the evenings as a nurse in the Scottish home of the royal family. This new employment offered lodging for Jean and her children as part of her compensation for nursing services and when combined with her wages from taking care of the two spinsters, Jean was able to earn enough money to adequately care for her family.

One evening, while Queen Victoria and Prince Albert were away from the palace, the servants decided they would let their children take turns sleeping in the king's bed. Although nervous, Jean took her turn and with her children, slept in the gigantic bed overnight. "Although I was very nervous and didn't sleep much at all," Jean recalled, "It was a wonderful opportunity for the children to know they had slept in the royal bed."

Jean maintained her employment with the two spinsters while she continued to work for the Queen. Over the weeks that passed since Janet expelled Jean from her home, the mother and daughter, thanks to Richard's intercession, began speaking and resolving their issues. Jean's brother Richard was a peacemaker and couldn't stand seeing his sister and mother separated from each other. While Jean still faced strong resistance from her mother, she maintained her commitment to join the Latter-day Saint Church. Her mother began to sense Jean's religious conviction and as she learned more about the church, her feelings softened.

Jean's profound belief in this new gospel compelled her to share her understanding of the church with her generous female employers, who openly inquired if joining this religion would involve a move to another city or take her away from her beloved Scotland. Jean told them that the church's prophet lived in America and that is where many other newly baptized members were emigrating. With the threat of losing their caretaker whom they'd grown to love, the two women deluged Jean with questions, not understanding why she would want to leave their employ and pursue a religious "feeling" halfway around the world. Hoping to keep Jean as their caretaker, the spinsters promised to make Jean the sole heir to their large estate if she would just remain with them in Scotland until their deaths. Although Jean had grown deeply fond of the women she cared for, she made no offers or commitments. As the weeks passed, the women hoped the religion issue had just been a fleeting thought and Jean had decided to stay. They felt it best to not ask any further questions and Jean avoided bringing up the topic again.

Each day, Jean looked forward to her discussions with the missionaries and met with them often; she even began planning a date to be baptized. One night, as she was listening to a discussion on the payment of tithes and offerings, Jean overheard mention of a program that the Church had instituted to help followers migrate from Europe to America, called the Perpetual Emigration Fund. She had been dreaming of joining the Saints in the church she had grown to love, and this program could make that a reality.

The Perpetual Emigration Fund (PEF) was one of the largest enterprises undertaken by the Latter-day Saint church in the nineteenth century. Beginning in 1850, the revolving (or perpetual) fund aided the poor, especially the European emigrants in securing passage to America, where they would join with thousands of other members who desired to live near the newly established headquarters of the church. Those recipients who were helped by the fund were expected to reimburse it after settling in the American West. PEF agents in Europe chartered ships, or special sections of ships, at reduced fares for emigrants. Other agents in New York, Boston, Philadelphia, New Orleans, and St. Louis helped make travel arrangements at reduced costs for the overland journey to Utah.

Jean had heard enough. She committed to a baptism and asked if she could begin making payments into the Perpetual Emigration

Fund to travel to America. Within a few days, she made her first installment. She broke the news to her mother that she had selected a date for baptism and invited her to attend. Surprisingly, Janet agreed and was present on Feb. 21, 1850 when Jean was baptized in the Green Oak Branch of Renfrewshire, becoming a member of The Church of Jesus Christ of Latter-day Saints. Elder Robert Gault performed the baptism, which was witnessed by two elders of the church alongside Janet, Richard, Joanna and Jean's three children. The witnesses at Jean's baptism remarked that the spirit they felt in the room during the ordinance was very special. Richard was especially touched by the service and shortly thereafter, invited the missionaries to teach him about the Church. It wasn't long before both Richard and Joanna joined Jean in church membership.

As it turned out, the minister's refusal to meet with the missionaries a few months earlier, and the feelings of regret and sadness Janet felt in sending her child and grandchildren into that stormy night, made it possible for Jean to convince her mother that the minister himself must not be sure of his beliefs. And, despite fifty years in the Presbyterian faith, Jean's mother Janet, eventually entered the waters of baptism and also joined the Saints. On many occasions, Jean's mother and siblings remarked that they could never have endured the many challenges they later faced in their lives had they not gained a "testimony" of the gospel's truthfulness, as the members called it.

Janet, Richard and Joanna also started making payments into the emigration fund as they too were determined to travel to America with Jean. Soon, Jean had deposited enough money in the fund that she and her children could make plans to leave Scotland forever. They, as well as Jean's mother, brother and her sister began the journey to America from Liverpool, England on September 4, 1850.

* * * * * *

Chattering prairie dogs peeking out from their labyrinth of underground burrows, lowing cattle and snorting horses mingled together and competed with chirping birds who welcomed the new day. These were the sounds that greeted Jane every morning. In awe of her life and surroundings, she would silently utter prayers of thanksgiving acknowledging the abundant blessings of life and the happiness she and Charles partook of each day. She was especially grateful for the comfortable family cabin that had been whittled out by her husband's hands from the timber of Blue Mountains.

Monticello's Blue Mountains had served as a life-saving landmark for early travelers navigating their way from the larger settlements some three hundred miles north in the Salt Lake Valley. It had also provided the settlers with much needed timber to build cabins, barns, dikes and fences and heat their homes throughout the long winter months. The Blue Mountains were life itself. Its dense forest, teemed with grouse, deer and elk, became food for pioneer tables. Throughout the summer, craftsmen would drive their horse-drawn buckboard wagons up the mountains where they laboriously sliced the large pine trees into usable logs. Up the mountain empty, then down heavy laden with bounty. The raw material would then be added to the structure and the of substance of lives lived in waiting at the foot of the mountain. It was terribly difficult work, yet every member of the community knew it was necessary for their very survival. Nature was self-serve or die.

After some quiet moments enjoying the beautiful epiphany of sunrise, Jane reminded herself to get busy, for there was much to be done. July 24th was an especially exciting day for members of the small community as well as the entire population of territorial Utah.

The annual holiday celebrated the Mormon pioneers' entry into the Salt Lake Valley in 1847. By 1891, 60,000 members of the church had migrated to Utah from all around the world. Faith had served as an enduring and binding bulwark against the ceaseless ravages of the frontier. Jane and Charles Walton were no exception. They both had traveled on foot for months crossing the American plains to join other Saints in Utah, a place then called The Deseret Territory.

As she returned to the cabin, Jane was greeted by her three grown children who ranged in age from nineteen to twenty-three years. Each had come to help with preparations for the big celebration that evening. For Charles Sr., today was a day of some rest from his many responsibilities. Not only had he continued to teach school and care for his farm and livestock, he was also serving as the postmaster for Monticello. The Walton children were still single and looked forward to the dance that night and the chance to mingle among the comely members of the opposite gender. The little children in the community anticipated playing tag, spitting watermelon seeds and playing on the rope swing by the riverbank. To the responsibility-ridden adults it was an opportunity to over-eat in these lean times and to step away from the dust and dirt of their daily work in favor of dancing, singing, playing games and of course, enjoying the smorgasbord of foods and treats prepared by friends and neighbors.

Jane busied herself at the sink, preparing vegetables and fruits. As she worked, she instinctively sang her favorite hymn, "I'll Go Where You Want Me To Go." The words reminded her of the convictions that had carried her to this place in her life.

"It may not be on the mountain height,
   Or over the stormy sea,
It may not be at the battle's front,
   My Lord will have need of me.
But if, by a still, small voice he calls,
   To paths that I do not know,
I'll answer, dear Lord, with my hand in thine:
   I'll go where you want me to go.

I'll go where you want me to go, dear Lord,
   Over mountain or plain or sea;
I'll say what you want me to say, dear Lord;
   I'll be what you want me to be."

Perhaps today there are loving words,
   Which Jesus would have me speak;
There may be now in the paths of sin,
   Some wand'rer whom I should seek.
O Savior, if thou wilt be my guide,
   Tho dark and rugged the way,
My voice shall echo the message sweet:
   I'll say what you want me to say.

There's surely somewhere a lowly place,
   In earth's harvest fields so wide
Where I may labor through life's short day,
   For Jesus, the Crucified.
So trusting my all to thy tender care,
   And knowing thou lovest me,
I'll do thy will with a heart sincere:
   I'll be what you want me to be.

There's surely somewhere a lowly place,
   In earth's harvest fields so wide
Where I may labor through life's short day,
   For Jesus, the Crucified.
So trusting my all to thy tender care,
   And knowing thou lovest me,
I'll do thy will with a heart sincere:
   I'll be what you want me to be.

Chapter Two
Farewell

Jane was almost four years old when her mother Jean packed up the family and began the voyage from Edinburgh, Scotland to Liverpool, England. On this relatively short leg of their journey to America the family enjoyed comfortable passage. Many of the local sights were exciting to see from the vantage point of the sea, but soon the familiarity of the landscape faded, as did the coastline of Scotland. Amid the excitement of traveling to a new home lurked quiet apprehension of the mysteries that awaited the travelers. England was a sister country to the family's native home, and they felt relatively safe among its people and culture.

As the group arrived in Liverpool, Jean and Janet were quick to remind the family that there was no time for "dilly dallying." There was much to be done, and first on the list was to locate the Perpetual Emigration agent from the Church who had written to inform them that he would be waiting for the family at the docks when they disembarked. Relieved, Jean saw the agent with a sign in his hand and introduced herself and her family. Before she could finish her introductions, the agent pointed to a corner of the dock and told the family to, "Wait right there," until everyone was gathered together. Jean appreciated the professionalism of the agent as she watched him gather his small flock of emigrants and surgically remove them from the crowds of people on the docks. One by one, she met other would-be travelers and together they dutifully stood in their appointed places at the docks corner, each waiting for further instructions.

The seaport of Liverpool had already witnessed thousands of emigrants walking its planks during the months that preceded the McKechnie's and Bee's trip to America. In fact, the London News had reported a few weeks earlier that nearly 92,000 emigrants had passed through Liverpool's gates every year for the preceding 25 years. Another article in the London News on July 6th, 1850 reported: "The emigration of the present year bids fair to exceed even the unprecedentedly large emigration of 1849. This human stream flows principally through the ports of London and Liverpool; as there is but little direct emigration from Scotland or Ireland." The news report continued by stating, "In the year 1849, out of the total number of 299,498 emigrants, more than one-half, or 153,902 left from the port of Liverpool."

The travelers didn't need the news reports to convince them that they were just another number among the roughly one thousand emigrants who crossed through the gates each day. They recognized that they needed to be ready at a moment's notice for instructions from the agent who scurried back and forth. Once he gathered everyone together, the representative began answering questions.

Many of the emigrants wondered what type of accommodations they would be enjoying on the trip across the ocean. In most cases, it hadn't been decided because the emigration agent didn't purchase tickets until the last possible moment, thus ensuring the best possible price. The choices were simply first or second-class cabins, and only a very few travelers ever enjoyed a first-class cabin. In 1849, only 4,639 first class cabins were booked out of the 154,000 people who sailed from the port of Liverpool.

One by one, the travelers' questions were answered, and the group prepared for a night or two of lodging while their individual assignments were made. Jean and her children, along with the other passengers, had a few hours to explore the port area of Liverpool while waiting for final instructions. While they waited, the agent from the church Perpetual Emigration Fund worked his magic in obtaining passage at the best possible price. The competition for fares was intense and an emigrant who was represented by an inexperienced guide, or those individuals who chose to book their own passage were often frustrated and taken advantage of. Jean and the others who had worked their passage through the Church, by comparison, had a rather pleasant experience. The cost of their lodging while they waited for the ship was reduced, and they had no need to worry about the hassle of purchasing their on-board accommodations at the most cost-efficient price. As the day passed, the fares fluctuated dramatically, and the agent watched closely, almost as if in tune with the ebb and flow of the industry, for the correct moment to book. Purchasing too soon would result in higher prices and buying a ticket too late could mean splitting up families, something that was rarely done. The difference in the fluctuating price of the steerage was significant and directly affected the agent's commission, thus, great care was taken during this negotiation process. Once bookings were made, it could be a matter of hours before the emigrant would be required to check in for the passage, or it could take days until they departed.

To pass the time, Jean and her children walked around the docks, and were mesmerized with the sights and sounds of Liverpool. They were accustomed to large shipping ports, having lived all their lives within walking distance of the ports of Edinburgh, yet Liverpool possessed an ambiance that demanded respect. The walls of the businesses that lined the docks and the shops near the port were covered with posters advertising the great adventures that awaited those who sailed. The words were large and carefully laid out on the posters to attract immediate attention. The images were captivating as they spoke of travel to various far-off lands, including of course, America. The competition for shipping vessels was great with many of the shipping leaders such as the New World, the Isaac Webb, the London or the Star of the West, each boasting their claim to the safest record and the modernized amenities onboard. Most of the larger vessels, primarily from America, could carry around 400 passengers.

Each morning, the Church's emigrants would gather at the dock for a short meeting with the agent who would report his progress in obtaining passage. There, the agent would also shout out the vessel assignments that had been made and begin the registration process before he returned to the bartering table for additional places on the ships throughout the day. It was on their second day at port that Jean learned that she and her family would be traveling on the North Atlantic, leaving September 3rd at 11:00 am, bound for the American city of New Orleans.

The passengers assigned to the North Atlantic had three days to prepare for the ship's departure. The next order of business was to see a local doctor and get clearance to travel across the ocean. By the terms of the New Passenger Act, enforced by the Medical Inspector's Office in England, "No passenger-ship was allowed to proceed until a medical practitioner appointed by the emigration office of the port shall have inspected the medicine-chest and passengers, and certified that the medicines etc. are sufficient, and that the passengers are free from contagious disease."

The travelers raced to the doctor and soon, with clearance papers in their hands, Jean's family presented their medical forms to the owner of the ship for admittance. The ship's owner had the responsibility of paying the medical inspector the sum of one sterling pound for every 100 people inspected. Having completed this process, the family had their passenger ticket stamped in the affirmative and they were instructed to show up three to four hours before the ship embarked on its journey.

With detailed plans in hand, including a boarding date and time, Jean took her children and joined her mother, sister and brother on a shopping trip into Liverpool to gather some last-minute items that might be needed on the trip. Small items of clothing, toiletries and medicines were priorities. Richard reviewed his possessions and made sure he had everything the ship rules would allow him to bring on board, including the additional items granted for male passengers. Men were allowed to bring a few necessary tools to aid in building a new life in American such as a saw, a wood plane, hammers, chisels and augers. Besides the tools, Richard could bring six shirts, six pairs of stockings, an extra pair of shoes and two complete suits of exterior clothing. The women and children were allowed to bring six simple dresses, two flannel petticoats, six pairs of stockings, two pairs of shoes and two gowns.

As Jean purchased the needed items, they learned from some of the more seasoned travelers that the government also allowed them to bring food and supplies to help them deal with the passage. By law, each passenger could bring two and one-half pounds of bread or biscuits, one pound of wheat flour, five pounds of oatmeal, two pounds of rice, two ounces of tea, one-half pound of sugar and one-half pound of molasses, which could be issued to the traveler as often as twice per week. Each traveler was also allotted up to three quarts of water per day. In some circumstances five pounds of potatoes could be substituted for one pound of oatmeal if the ship originated from either Irish or Scottish ports. Jean's family was fortunate enough to be on a ship with over 100 passengers. Because of this, the law provided that they would have an experienced cook with the appropriate cooking utensils on board their vessel as well.

On September 3rd, 1850, the passengers of the North Atlantic stood at the doorway ramp ready to board. It was 7:00 am, exactly four hours before the ship was to leave the Waterloo dock at Liverpool. Uniformed members of the ship's staff hustled to and fro as shouts from the lieutenants could be heard from the boarding area. "Prepare to receive the passengers," shouted one lieutenant while several muscular and tattooed staff members lowered long, wide planks from the swaying ship's stable foundation of the port. On the upper deck, just above the plank where passengers would board the ship, stood a middle-aged man with a short, white beard. He was dressed in a white uniform that was neatly pressed. His cap fit snuggly to his head with the brim just inches from his nose. His eyes, shadowed by the bill of the cap, seemed strong and focused. As the ship's crew passed the man, many stopped and received instruction, often saluting him as they departed. This was Captain John Henry Cook, an American trained sailor who had sailed the Atlantic many times before. Rumors among the passengers suggested that he had also commanded many ships as a naval officer, protecting American shores. His very presence and stature brought a sense of security to Jean and the others.

Once everyone was loaded on the ship it was finally time to depart Great Britain forever. Janet, Richard, Joanna, Jean, Georgina, Jane and John stood quietly on the deck of the North Atlantic as the large ropes that held the ship to the docks were tossed aside. Bellowing smoke and loud rumbling noises erupted as the steam ship pulled away from the wooden docks. Many of the passengers waved goodbye to friends and loved ones who, in turn, waved from the docks, shouting, "bon' voyage," and "goodbye." As Jane glanced over to her mother and grandmother, she noticed tears in their eyes, and she knew they both realized they would probably never see their homeland again. Jean remembered something she read in the newspaper in Liverpool just days before, "The last look, if known to be the last, is always sorrowful, and refuses, in most instances, to see the wrong and the suffering, the error and the misery, which may have impelled the one who takes it, to venture from the old into the new, from the tried to the untried path, and to recommence existence under new auspices, and with new and totally different prospects."

Registered on the passenger list of the North Atlantic were many Latter-day Saint converts from Great Britain. Included on the list were Jean Bee, (age 23), her mother Janet (age 52), her sister Joanna (age 21) and her brother Richard (age 15). They stood proudly among the passengers along with Jean's young family consisting of Georgina (age 5), Jane (age 4) and John (age 1-1/2).

The North Atlantic was slowly pulled away from the docks of Liverpool and then south along the Mersey River by a small, yet powerful tugboat. The waving handkerchiefs, the raised hats and open palms slowly disappeared as the ship sailed away. The tugboat would tow the large ship for over 5 miles until the massive craft could safely assume control on its own in the open waters of the Atlantic. As the tugboat pulled, prodded and churned its way along the Mersey, the crew of the ship assembled the passengers together in order to hold the second roll call of the paying passengers and conduct a search for stowaways. Because of the cost of ocean travel, the practice of 'stowing away', or hiding inside the ship until all the tickets for travel had been collected, was becoming a common problem and every ship's employee went to great lengths to minimize the number of freeloaders on each crossing. The sea hands considered it a challenge to find stowaways before the ship hit open water, but most often, it was days into the voyage before most were discovered. Sometimes, the stowaways would gain access onto the ship by concealing themselves in trunks, barrels, and chests or in the many nooks and crannies of the ship's construction. Usually, air holes on shipping containers raised enough suspicion that the stowaways were captured quite quickly. Some freeloaders hid in barrels of salt or grains. When suspected, the shipmates would turn the barrels upside down and listen for the screams as the hitchers were turned on their head and the air space around their faces filled with grain. Unfortunately, there had been cases of dead stowaways being discovered well into the trip, having never escaped their confines.

If the intruders could be found soon enough, they would usually be returned to dry land to face criminal charges. If found later at sea, some ship captains would deal with the matter in a much crueler manner. Stowaways could be tarred and feathered or made to remain on the upper decks of the ship without adequate clothing against the cold of the seas. In most cases, they would be forced to do manual labor on board, usually with unpleasant jobs such as cleaning human and animal waste.

At the captain's order, the sailors would take a careful inventory of every passenger in a very organized manner. As each cabin of passengers was called upon, the occupants would file into the quarterdeck for counting. When passengers reached the deck, they would file past a clerk and then the ship's surgeon who would call for their ticket. As the travelers handed their tickets to the clerk, the surgeon would quickly inspect each passenger once more. Mistakes at this point were costly because once the vessel arrived in New Orleans, the ship's owner would have to pay a poll-tax of one and one-half dollars per passenger. If any of the passengers were found to be deformed or helpless, the owners of The North Atlantic would be fined $75 for bringing the person to America. The handicapped individual would then have to sign a bond stating that they would not become a burden on the public—otherwise, they would not be admitted. Jean and her family were relieved that they were quickly processed and allowed to return to the security and privacy of their berths.

Having passed inspection, the family was now officially passengers of The North Atlantic, a new class of steamship that had the ability to rely on sail for power when needed. She was a state-of-the-art ship, having been constructed only a year earlier, yet she was still made largely of wood, and she creaked noisily. Amid the uncertainty of ocean travel, there was a great deal of excitement as the small group began their much-anticipated journey. None of the travelers seemed to have any inkling of the dangers that lay ahead in the open seas. Had they known of the terrible disasters that would befall many of the ships during the second half of the 19th century, they may have turned back immediately.

One such ship, the President, set sail from New York headed to Liverpool in 1841 with 136 persons on board. That vessel belonged to the unlucky British and American Steam Navigation Company that had many unsuccessful voyages. When the ship sailed back to New York, she encountered gale force winds and disappeared into the dark waters. Everyone on board perished with her, including the son of the Duke of Richmond and a well-known Irish comedian of the day named Tyrone Power, an ancestor of the American actor of the same name.

Far more terrible was the fate of a vessel named the City of Glasgow, which was used for trading between Glasgow and New York. She was a beautiful craft built on Scotland's River Clyde. She weighed 1600 tons and was believed to be able to stand the fury of the Atlantic Ocean. In addition to her large engines, she could carry an enormous amount of canvas sails. On March 1, 1854 she set sail with 480 persons aboard, but was, tragically, never heard from again.

In the 1850's an Atlantic shipping company known as the Collins Line constructed two paddle steamers named Arctic and Pacific. Each vessel cost nearly 200,000 pounds each. On September 27, 1854 the Arctic collided with a small French steamer off the coast of Newfoundland. Three hundred and twenty-two lives were lost including the managing director of the company, Mr. Collins and his wife, son and daughter.

Later, the steamship Tempest, of the Anchor Line, was added to the increasing list of mysterious disappearances in the Atlantic Ocean. She sailed in February of 1875 with a crew and passenger list numbering 150. She, also, was never seen again. The Anchor Line also produced the steamer, United Kingdom. It too disappeared with 80 people on board in 1868.

Over the next 20 years, 18 other ships were victims of similar seafaring disasters. The Naronic, which was touted as a reliable and sturdy twin-screw cargo vessel, also disappeared. This ship had been built to withstand any gale and its disappearance created a profound sensation in the industry.

The journey across the Atlantic Ocean was most certainly a dangerous one. The ferocious waters overwhelmed many steamships; other vessels went down quickly after colliding with icebergs and submerged derelicts. The passengers aboard the North Atlantic would not have known how comparatively fortunate and seemingly blessed their ocean hop would be. Through the years, The Latter-day Saint faithful seemed to enjoy mostly favorable Atlantic crossings. Their impressive record was taken as a faith-affirming sign that led to rumors of a shipping maxim to include "Mormons" on board any trip for good luck. The Saints attributed their remarkable safety record to the hand of Providence and the fact that the ships were often dedicated and blessed before embarking on the voyage.

One disaster involving church members, however, was recorded. The American vessel, The Julia Ann, cast off from Sydney, Australia bound for San Francisco in 1855. There were 56 people on board, including crew members and members of the founding families of the Latter-day Saint Church in Australia. The Julia Ann was considered a "light and seaworthy bark." Its cargo included 350 tons of coal.

As the voyage began, passengers gathered to sing a traditional embarking song, "The Gallant Ship is Under Way." As the passengers began to realize the nearly 3-month voyage that lay ahead of them, their singing sounded more like a funeral dirge than a celebratory song. On October 3rd, after some 27 days at sea, Captain Benjamin Franklin Pond became deeply concerned as the ship approached the uninhabited Isles of Scilly. The islands were surrounded by dangerous and poorly mapped reefs. After a nerve-wracking day, Captain Pond presumed the reefs were past and went below for some rest. Neither stars nor moon were visible that dark night.

At about 8:30 p.m. a cry was heard: "Hard down the helm!" At that moment, the heavily laden Julia Ann thundered headlong into a coral reef leaving a gaping hole that continued to widen beneath. Heavy waves relentlessly pounded the vessel sideways against the reef. Indescribable confusion followed as mothers snatched their children from their slumbers and held them in their arms screaming and lamenting. The vessel was not sinking—it was breaking up on the reef.

Two young girls, Mary Humphreys and Marian Anderson, were washed off the deck and were seen no more. Other passengers, bruised and soaking wet, clung to the deck, as they dodged wildly swinging booms. Elder John McCarthy, a missionary, said, "I saw mothers nursing their babes in the midst of falling masts and broken spars while the breakers were rolling twenty feet high over the wreck." The lifeboats, useless in the rocks and waves, were torn loose. A crewmember volunteered to swim to the reef in search of firm footing. He managed somehow to fasten a rope to a rock while women and children were evacuated. Eliza Harris strapped her 6-month-old son, Lister, to her breast to go to the rocks when a huge wave struck the ship, tearing up the bulwarks and threatening death and destruction to everything within reach. The Julia Ann broke in half across the hatch. Eliza and her son were swept from the deck and drowned. Martha Humphreys, the mother of Mary, was also swept from the deck to drown. At a critical point, waves pulled the ship back toward open waters. The rope that had been fastened to the rock snapped, and those still on the ship appeared doomed. The ship began to break into more pieces and the deck separated from the heavy, coal-filled cargo hold and washed high onto the rocks, the coal headed elsewhere.

The ordeal lasted three long hours. Fifty-one cold and wet survivors waited out the night. As dawn broke across the horizon, the folks despaired when no land could be seen. But, as the sun rose higher, crewmembers spotted a distant barren island—essentially a large sand bar—and a few crewmen managed to reach it on a badly leaking lifeboat they'd recovered and patched. Others waited on the reef encircled by sharks, with no drinking water, and clothing torn to shreds. As soon as the women and children were carried by boat to the island, the remaining men pulled towing rafts along the miles-long underwater reef. They swam over gaps in the reef and scrambled on the rafts when sharks came too close. On one occasion, the men counted 20 sharks. After hours of struggle and a day, a night and a day, without drinking water, they arrived on the island. Luckily, on the island, children found holes in the sand where fresh water seeped. The survivors subsisted for two months on turtle meat and eggs, shellfish and sharks. Water was collected in coconuts and a barrel embedded in shallow wells. The women made a type of pancake from shredded coconut, and turtle eggs mixed with flour.

Captain Pond had been able to save his navigational instruments and determined the group's location. Far from ship routes and inhabited islands, he estimated they were 300-500 miles west of the Society Islands (French Polynesia). Rescue was out of the question. Pond's crew would have to go for help. On Dec. 2, 1855, after four days of rowing to the east and 60 days after the shipwreck, the men sighted a schooner, the Emma Packer. The schooner rescued the shoeless, nearly bare and destitute company, and arrived in Tahiti Dec. 19th. All of the original survivors of the wreck eventually found passage from Tahiti to their various destinations. The Church members made their way to San Francisco and most of them subsequently trekked east to the Great Basin.

Chapter Three
Seafarer

Most of the travelers aboard The North Atlantic were unaware of the disappearance of ships at sea and were naïve to the dangers of ocean travel. The ship's crew was careful that no discussion was made of such events. Extra care was taken to ensure the children on board remained innocent to the tragedies they very well could encounter while at sea. Jean and Janet were committed to regarding the journey as an adventure of hope and excitement, rather than one of fear. Along with study times, church and play time, each day was full of chores and tasks. By order of the Ship Master, every passenger had to agree to a written, "Rules for Passengers" order that originated from an abstract of the Queen's Order in Council on October 6, 1849. The rules were designed to preserve order and secure cleanliness and adequate ventilation on board passenger ships.

The order required every passenger to rise at 7:00 am unless they were otherwise permitted to stay in bed by the ship's surgeon. Breakfast was to be eaten between 8:00 am and 9:00 am. Dinner was served at 1:00 pm and supper began at 6:00 pm. Each passenger was expected to eat their meals in their own sleeping berth and to clean their own plate and utensils. While some rules were not questioned, this requirement was by far one of the most controversial. It was understood that the ship could quickly become a breeding ground for pests if passengers were allowed to eat wherever they pleased, and there was no space for a designated dining room on the already-full vessel, but the passengers complained, nonetheless. The sleeping berth was of course where travelers slept, as well as played and lived every day of their journey across the ocean and passengers could see that eating on their beds through rough waters would most certainly be unsanitary.

Other rules, such as those dealing with fires, didn't seem to be questioned. The passengers all knew that they were traveling on a ship made of wood and that fires had to be strictly controlled. They had to rely on the "passenger cook" for their meals and it was against the ship's rules for anyone to go into the kitchen without express permission of the ship's master. Only the passenger's cook could light a fire which would happen each morning at 7:00 am and he was responsible to watch and keep the flame alive until 7:00 pm, at which time it would be extinguished. At times, the shipmaster could authorize additional time for the cook's light, in circumstances such as caring for the sick, but it was rare that the rule was ever adjusted.

The family was glad that they were traveling during the time of year when there was plenty of light in the sky. But as September came to a close, October brought fewer daylight hours. At dusk, members of the ship's staff lit three safety lamps. One of the three lights could be kept burning all night in the main hatchway but the other two needed to be extinguished by 10:00 pm. Never were naked lights, or lights without shields, allowed on the ship for any reason, and loose hay and straw was never allowed below the deck. An accidental fire could easily ignite the oil-soaked timbers of the ship, sending hundreds of people into the watery grasp of the ocean, if not strictly controlled.

Each morning, the passengers were required to complete certain chores before eating breakfast. At the crack of dawn, as the travelers got out of their beds, they were required to dress themselves and then roll up their beds and sweep the decks, including the space under the bottom of the berths. The dirt that was collected was to be thrown overboard, and this task often fell on little Jane and Georgina. The first time Jane threw the dirt over the rail, a stiff wind blew it back into her face and onto the ship's deck. She never made that mistake again, but carefully analyzed the wind's direction before dumping her load.

Once the individual berths were cleaned, it was incumbent upon everyone to clean the common areas of the ship. The "sweepers for the day" were assigned in rotation, with five sweepers per 100 passengers. Only male passengers over the age of 14 were used for this duty and Jane, Georgina or John never had to fulfill this role. They did, however, see their Uncle Richard perform it on many occasions. When it was his assigned turn, Richard would join four other men in cleaning the ladders, the hospital and dining rooms. After each meal, Richard would take a soft stone called a "dry holy stone," and scrub the decks of the ship. Older seafaring workers taught Richard that the Royal Navy used the stones which originally came from the St. Nicholas Church in Great Yarmouth. He was required to scrub the deck of the ship with the stone while on his knees, as if in prayer. Since he was younger, he was given a smaller stone, called a "prayer book". The older men were given larger stones referred to as "Bibles." It seemed Richard was becoming a religious person after all, one way or another.

The "sweepers" would only clean the common areas of the ship and the occupants of each berth were responsible to make sure the berth was well brushed out. Single women were ordered to keep their own compartment clean and orderly. Every one of the passengers, including children, was required to regularly take their bedding to the upper decks and air them out by shaking them. Every Monday and Tuesday were designated as wash days, but the passengers were warned that no clothing was to be washed or dried between decks, only on the upper deck. The smell on board the ship would become unbearable at times and it was important that the scuttle and stern ports of the ship remained open from 7:00 am until 10:00 pm, unless the weather was bad. The hatches on the ship also needed to be open at all times. There was a toilet on the ship for women and children only. The men and boys onboard had to go to the top deck and use the "head", a toilet situated where the winds would blow the smell away from the ship while providing some protection and shelter.

Jean and her children, like the other emigrants on board the ship, spent the majority of their time confined to their quarters between the decks of the ship. They read, played, ate and slept in the small spaces they were allotted. From time to time, a group of men would get together to play cards and invariably a friendly game would turn to one form or another of gambling. This would lead to fighting, swearing, and riotous behavior that was instantly dealt with by the Master. When the passengers had boarded The North Atlantic, any swords or weapons, along with any gunpowder or alcohol, had been seized until the completion of the voyage. Thus, rarely did a disagreement progress beyond a black eye or a swollen lip.

Jean found much of the voyage to be a test of sheer will. Much of her time was spent below deck, in the often-stifled air, entertaining her children. When she wasn't helping them with their individual chores, she was reading with them. One of the children's favorite activities was climbing to the top deck with Jean, to see the never-ending ocean and feel the fresh sea breeze blowing in their faces. To the eyes of a child, the world was vast, and innumerable fantasies were imagined beneath the surface of the water, and in the boundless sky.

Jean was deeply grateful for the ship's rules regarding the weekly observance of the Sabbath. Each passenger was expected to "muster," or, gather together, by ten o'clock in the morning wearing "clean and decent apparel." Once assembled, a short sermon would be given, and the remainder of the day was to be "observed as religiously as circumstances would admit." For Jean, this was a day to concentrate on her new religion and to spend time reading the scriptures and discussing God. She enjoyed the opportunity to get dressed up and felt that everyone on board acted a little more civil on Sundays.

When the weather was bad, the ship would creak and groan under the stress of the rough seas. In these conditions, most of the passengers would get seasick and lie in the dark enduring the stench while praying for the storm to end. They could then enjoy a short break on the upper deck to breathe the fresh sea air. When one passenger became sick enough to vomit, others would quickly follow suit, so everyone did all they could to keep those around them from getting ill. Cleanliness was one of the most important issues onboard and drinking plenty of water helped curb sickness. The ship's surgeon carried approximately 10 pounds of arrowroot, 50 pounds of preserved beef, 400 pints of lemon juice, 400 pounds of sugar, 60 pounds of scotch barley, 18 bottles of port wine, 50 gallons of rum and 300 gallons of stout per 100 passengers to aid in caring for the sick. Alcohol also nursed many illnesses at sea.

After several weeks at sea, a 63-year-old woman on the North Atlantic, named Betty Hulme, became deathly ill. To the members of the 2nd class cabins, this was upsetting news indeed. They had grown to love and rely upon each other as if they were family, so it was no surprise the women of the 2nd class cabins rallied together to help care for Betty, including Jean, Janet, and Joanna. Over the course of a few days, Betty became dehydrated and much sicker. When the news came several days later that Mrs. Hulme had passed away, it sent shockwaves of sadness through the passengers. It was announced that Betty would be buried at sea later that day, prompting the passengers to join Captain Cook in preparing a funeral service for their departed friend. At the appointed hour, the captain stood at the quarterdeck on the port side of the ship with Mrs. Hulme's body wrapped in a white sheet in front of him. The passengers from the ship were invited to attend a short memorial service and each dressed in their finest Sunday worship clothes.

Captain Cook recited the Twenty Third Psalm from the Bible, "The Lord is my shepherd: I shall not want… Yea, though I walk through the valley of the shadow of death, I will fear no evil: for thou art with me, thy rod and staff they comfort me… Surely goodness and mercy shall follow me all the days of my life: and I will dwell in the house of the Lord forever." Captain Cook then instructed the sailors to lower Mrs. Hulme's body into the choppy water below for a traditional burial at sea. Jane was in her Uncle Richard's arms as she witnessed the final stages of the burial. Suddenly, all were horrified to see several large sharks strike and then fight over the body that had been deposited in their waters. Richard, Jane and a host of others watched as Mrs. Hulme's body was devoured.

Within a few days of Mrs. Hulme's death and burial, three-year old Katren Bonner, a friend of Jane's and a playmate on board the ship, also died from dehydration caused by prolonged vomiting. She had been sick for several days and as her condition worsened, she slipped into a coma. The child quietly went to sleep and then died. Jane was too young to understand why her playmate had died and became terrified at the thought of another burial at sea, remembering the horror of sharks attacking Mrs. Hulme's body. During this funeral, Captain Cook made sure that Katren was tightly wrapped and heavily weighted before dropping her into the dark and deep waters of the Atlantic.

In the ninth week of the voyage, the North Atlantic entered the Gulf of Mexico. The ship suddenly began to encounter engine trouble and to make matters worse, there was no wind to propel the ship under sail. As the vessel sat motionless on the open sea, Richard approached one of the sailors and said, "We are rocking in the bosom of the deep. Things are monotonous and I was wondering if it would be alright if us boys would venture and have a swim?" Richard's request was ignored until one sailor agreed to represent the boys in asking permission of the captain of the ship. To their surprise, Captain Cook gave permission and personally delivered the message stating, "You can go swimming off the ship provided only one of you goes in at a time. There are sharks in the locality, and I don't want to be liable for such an accident."

Richard was selected to be the first to enter the waters and he was keen to the idea, having grown up in the port region of Edinburgh. Later, Richard recalled, "I was not afraid of the water, having been raised as it were by the seashore and in the water most every day. I stripped and sprang overboard and swam about thirty or forty yards from the vessel when the cry, 'Shark!' rang out." Two sailors sitting high above the upper decks of the vessel, spotted the predator just seconds after Richard dove into the water. "I can see his dorsal fin about 30 yards away, quick, get out!" yelled one of the sailors. Richard swam toward the ship as fast as he could while Janet screamed from her vantage point on the deck. Horrified passengers gathered at the scene remembering Mrs. Hulme's sea burial, only days earlier. Richard grabbed the ship's rope and climbed from the water as a large shark made a failed strike for him. One of the sailors who was hanging over the side of the ship trying to help yelled out, "He missed your foot by four inches." Janet ran to Richard as he climbed onto the ship and was so overcome with emotion that she couldn't express herself. Richard hugged his mother with one arm as he looked over his left shoulder at the monster below. The rush of adrenaline made him feel more like a hero at that moment than the lucky survivor of a near fatal shark attack, yet he was still shaking as he reflected on the experience. The shark was estimated to be about 15 feet in length, and it continued to circle the area for several minutes. The sailors attempted to harpoon it, even striking it several times, but the huge predator managed to get away. From that moment forward, no one was allowed to swim in the water and Richard enjoyed a great sense of accomplishment in his one and only swim in the Gulf of Mexico.

Within a few hours of the terrifying shark experience, the North Atlantic fell victim to a violent hurricane. Over the course of the next three days, the ship was driven back into the Atlantic Ocean, more than 300 miles off course. The storm was so strong that it tossed the ship continuously and the sounds inside the passenger berths were deafening and frightening. The normal creaks and groans of the ship gave way to loud crashing as the waves rolled over the top of the ship's deck. All of the hatchways were ordered closed and within a few hours, the steerage became stifling. Some of the passengers started feeling sick in the turbulent conditions. As the ship pitched to and fro under the powerful surge of the wind and waves, many more became ill and many began vomiting. Passengers thought they would suffocate from the horrible smells, yet most were so frightened by the pitching and wailing of the ship itself, that fear for their actual survival took precedence over sickness. To her children, Jean seemed unnerved by the crashing and motion of the ship. With each terrible crash, she tried to divert the children's attention by singing and playing games. Praying, however, calmed the family more than any diversion.

As the storm continued into the second day, Captain Cook called for all of the adult men on board the ship to report for duties to assist the crew. There was no time for eating or sleeping. The men were directed to begin bailing water by hand. And when they were not manning the pumps, they were repairing areas of damage or treating the wounds of injured sailors. As the strength of the crew and male passengers wore thin, Captain Cook solicited help from the women on board as well. Jean was busy caring for her children, but Janet and Joanna joined the men in bailing water and caring for crew members. Finally, at the end of the second day, the ship broke free of the hurricane and resumed her course westward toward New Orleans. Once the ship was settled into calmer seas, the passengers were finally allowed to exit their airless and muggy quarters. Jean escorted Georgina, Jane and John to the upper deck of the ship and together they breathed in the fresh air and caught their first view of American soil.

After 11 weeks at sea, the North Atlantic finally entered the mouth of the Mississippi River where it was met by tugboats and pilot boats that guided it into the New Orleans port. The family was finally able to set foot on American soil—their dream, although only half complete, had become a reality.

Chapter Four
The Mighty Mississippi

As fall came to a close in 1850, young Jane joined the ranks of seasoned travelers to claim victory over the great Atlantic Ocean, but it was only the beginning of a life of challenges for Jane. The terribly long journey across the ocean was now just a memory for the hardened passengers of the North Atlantic. The memories would elicit various emotions for each of the passengers. For some, the experience would invoke a memory of pride and accomplishment, having survived the many weeks at sea. For others, the recollections would summon harrowing sorrow as they stepped on American soil with members of their families missing. Relatives of those lost at sea would not have a plot of ground or a gravestone to mark the death of their loved one; the ocean had become their cemetery.

Even though she was only a child, Jane's emotional survival instincts began to develop in the face of the hardships she had endured at sea. She was being prepared for the life unfolding before her and she learned to live with the ever-present threat of death. Her mother's example of faith gave assurance to Jane and kept her world aligned. Jane had learned a valuable lesson on her Atlantic voyage—that faith and determination were essential to an individual's will in accomplishing a desired goal. This lesson would surely be relied upon time and again as she transitioned from seafarer to ground pounder. Those who traveled across the ocean and walked the plains in the 19th century were tested, tempered and validated by the obstacles they tackled—if they survived. Those who passed these overwhelming tests never complained about the hardships they endured. Instead, they acknowledged the hand of God in their victories.

After months at sea, the arrival in the Port of New Orleans was a welcomed relief. The shipyard was active, bustling with excitement as crowds of people made their way into the city which had become a chosen port for travelers during those early years of ocean faring. The New Orleans' port was preferred because of its size and the fact that it was a less-expensive, all-water route to other major destinations in America. For Jane and her family, the next stop along their westward journey would be Winter Quarters, Iowa, some 1,200 miles up the mighty Mississippi River. Winter Quarters was the staging area for the Saints as they prepared to move westward.

Jean's family filed off The North Atlantic and were met by another agent of the Perpetual Emigration Fund who helped them obtain their luggage and escorted them to a nearby hotel where they would spend the next three nights before departing for St. Louis. Usually, new arrivals were kept onboard the ship for several days while the next leg of their journey was secured. To the pleasure of the McKechnie's, their wait occurred on stable ground, in nice accommodations, complete with fresh linen and a bath. The family was excited as they got to the hotel for their first night in a full-size bed. However, after weeks of being rocked from side to side, they felt as if they were still at sea when they closed their eyes.

For three wonderful days, the explorers were charmed by the sights and sounds of the city of New Orleans. The music, dress and mannerisms of their American hosts were intriguing and at times captivating. Having come from the large city of Edinburgh, the city of New Orleans seemed manageable and almost familiar. New Orleans had doubled its population since the 1830s and was now the wealthiest and third-most populous city in America, yet it was also a city fraught with trouble. It had become a huge slave market with more than 650,000 slaves being brought to the Deep South through her ports. Sadly, owning humans represented more than a half a billion dollars in industry. Businesses sprang up in New Orleans in support of the sale of slaves, which included marketing, transportation, housing and clothing fees. Already sides were being taken on the abominable issue of slavery in America and whether it should be abolished or not, but for now, sadly, it existed.

While the children toured the city of New Orleans in the care of Richard and Joanna, Jean and Janet continued to work out their continued passage with the PEF agent in America. They reviewed their receipts and travel documents carefully and selected a steamboat named Pacific as their vessel. It would carry them north, up the Mississippi, to St. Louis, Missouri, and then on to Winter Quarters, near Omaha, Nebraska. While in Liverpool Jean had secured cabin accommodations for the Mississippi River trip at an additional cost. Most passengers paid $2.50 for the trip but Jane was able to afford the additional cost of $3.00 per person in order to have sleeping quarters. Those who were unable to pay the extra money or who booked their trip too late, couldn't get the more desirable accommodations and were classified as "deck passengers," or passengers without beds or shelter. Many of the deck passengers suffered from cholera and other illnesses.

With only a day left to prepare for the trip upriver, Jean and Janet shopped for some last-minute items. Powdered sugar cost four cents per pound, rice sold for one cent per pound and butter required 12 and one-half cents per pound. Together, they purchased $2.85 worth of supplies. Janet saw a fancy pair of boots, which were on sale for $16. After trying them on twice, she returned them to the rack saying, "They won't last on a walk to Salt Lake." After another day in New Orleans the family loaded their possessions onto the steamship and prepared for the river trip northward.

On November 4th, 1850, the steamship Pacific left New Orleans and began its journey up the Mississippi River, piloted by Captain Fithian. The travelers enjoyed a smooth ride up the river and noticed how stable the steamship seemed on the water's surface in comparison to the ocean journey they had just completed. The McKechnie's enjoyed seeing land on both sides of the ship and especially appreciated the fact that there were no sharks in the mighty Mississippi. As the noise of New Orleans faded into the background on the forest lined river, the passengers watched gulls flying alongside the ship, darting into the river where they splashed forcefully and then took flight again, usually with a fish in their beaks.

Occasionally, in order to get additional food, supplies, and fuel for the trip, the large steamship would pull to the side of the river next to a settlement with a dock that was large enough to accommodate and hold the ship in place. Whenever time allowed, the passengers would go ashore to purchase goods. With the recent completion of the year's harvest, many vegetables and fruits were available for purchase and several of the ship's passengers scurried to the markets in hopes of buying fresh produce—something they hadn't eaten in months.

Jean grew to love the short excursions off the ship, and found she enjoyed talking to the local residents milling about in the markets. The vendors seemed grateful to have the steamship's passengers flooding their markets with money, as well as the opportunity to trade cultures and learn about each other's lives. Jean recalled being told on multiple occasions how lucky her family was to be traveling upriver during November, when the temperatures were still mild and enjoyable but too cold for mosquitoes. The beautiful colors of autumn were almost gone and in many places the trees were leafless as "mother nature" continued her preparations for the long winter ahead.

While Jean enjoyed her time off the ship, Richard enjoyed sitting on the upper decks and watching the beautiful homes lining the river slide by as the boat continued its sluggish journey. As the days passed, he became deeply troubled by the sheer number of slave plantations he observed. His concern drove him to speak to the working sailors about the slaves and was in turn told that a good slave could be purchased for $25 and were used to do most of the hard labor in the fields. This struck a chord with Richard. The idea of owning a person challenged every moral fiber in his body, and the nonchalant nature of the sailors infuriated him. As their argument elevated, Richard and the sailors were suddenly tossed violently to the floor of the ship. The steamship had run aground in the middle of the Mississippi river.

For the captain of a riverboat, judging the water's depth and anticipating changes was a never-ending challenge. Heavy rains could send large volumes of water and debris from nearby tributaries into the Mississippi, creating deposits of sand and water that would change the river's floor. With an ever-changing river, 'running aground' was never explicitly frowned upon by experienced captains; 'running aground' in the same place twice, however, would often herald criticism.

As luck would have it on this particular night, another steamship was passing on its downstream run. The captain of the passing ship dropped his anchor and offered assistance. Together, the sailors and many of the male passengers on the ship, including Richard, worked into the night digging out the vessel. By daybreak, the steamship was back on water and forging up the river.

Over the days that followed, the ship ran aground several more times, though in each of those circumstances, the captain was able to reverse the motors and release the steamship. Word spread throughout the ship that the water on the Mississippi River was dangerously low and the ship's progress would be slowed if not halted altogether. Although these challenges beleaguered the crew, unfortunately a few of the weaker passengers who had survived the ocean crossing, suddenly died. The ship's carpenter built coffins for the deceased and a group of ten or twelve men carried the wood boxes into the woods that lined the river and buried them. Often, the caskets had to be weighted to keep them from floating out of the soil when the water table was high.

After several more days of slow travel, the steamship made its way into St. Louis. The intention of the captain and crew was to take the boat all the way to Council Bluffs, Iowa and then on to Winter Quarters, but the Missouri River was too low for navigation. The trip to Winter Quarters would have to wait for several months until the spring runoff waters could make their way down to the Missouri and

Mississippi River and into St. Louis. Unexpectedly, the passengers and supplies that were on the steamship were unloaded in St. Louis.

Once free of her tonnage, the steamship slowly crept southward down the river and back to New Orleans. Bewildered, Jane's family stood on the docks of St. Louis clutching their luggage, along with many other families who were just as confused. The family waited patiently to speak to the Perpetual Emigration Agent, wondering what lay in store for them. Soon, they learned they would be able to stay with other families who had preceded them in the voyage to St. Louis and that they would either have to find a way to get to Winter Quarters by rail or wait until the following spring. The McKechnie's decided to look for work and spend the winter in the city.

St. Louis was experiencing rapid growth in 1850. One of the major reasons was the influx of large numbers of immigrants, particularly from Germany and Ireland. German immigrants, often fleeing conflict and revolution in their homeland, came to St. Louis and its surrounding communities hoping to make a new life for themselves. St. Louis became a melting pot of cultures, and the two that seemed to take the strongest hold on the city were the German culture and the "Mormon" culture. Whereas, the German influence was seen in the written language, the "Mormon" influence was seen in the sheer number of Latter-day Saints that walked the streets. As the family began to settle into the new city, a sense of comfort came over them—they were among others just like them. Of course, the comfort wasn't permanent. It was quickly replaced with the stress of locating work. The need to obtain a paying job was imperative for securing their winter lodging and funding the next leg of the trip to Council Bluffs and Winter Quarters.

Richard was fortunate in securing employment with the help of John T. Caine, an elder in the Latter-day Saint Church, who used his influence to get Richard a job in a wholesale and retail grocery store. He was able to live with the owner of the grocery store and remained employed there through the winter. Meanwhile, Janet and Jean found work doing domestic cleaning and childcare. They were able to earn enough money to pay for their expenses throughout the winter and cover the final costs to bring their family to Winter Quarters in 1851. This was made possible, in part, because Richard was able to take home fruits and vegetables that otherwise would be tossed out from the grocery store. From time to time, Richard could secure a soup bone or butcher scraps that Jean could use to make tasty stews or soups. During that same winter, Joanna found lodging with a German family. They were kind and welcomed her in with open arms, but while Joanna only spoke English, the family only spoke German. Though the family had begun to form a caring relationship with Joanna, she soon found it best to find another place to stay.

Throughout the winter, Jean collected discarded and worn coats of soldiers who were passing through St. Louis and used the cloth and pieces of leather to make shoes for Jane, Georgina and John. While there was scarcely enough money to live on, Jean and Janet were successful in stretching and fashioning their goods for the benefit of their entire family. When others may have cursed the heavens for the challenges they were facing, Jean, her mother, and their combined children made sure that they thanked God daily for the bounty they enjoyed.

Richard enjoyed the area but was disturbed as he continued to witness the sale of many African slaves at public auctions held in the marketplace. So troubled was Richard, that he recorded the following in his journal, "While in St. Louis I witnessed the sale at public auction of many negro slaves exhibited in the marketplace and bartered off to the highest bidder, with no consideration being made as to family ties, but separated at the will of the auctioneer and purchaser in spite of the protests and cries of the unfortunate victims. Families were separated with no sympathy from the sellers." The terrible treatment he witnessed of these men and women remained a tender issue for Richard throughout his life and he was always quick to stand in defense of those who seemed defenseless.

While Richard was working at the store, Caine learned more about the young man's education and background and offered him employment as a journalist for the Missouri Republican Newspaper. The possibility of being a journalist was very interesting to Richard, but before he could make his decision, he was introduced to a man named Orson Hyde who worked in the printing business. As Richard and Orson became more acquainted, Hyde became aware of Richard's ability to write legibly and he liked the way Richard composed his thoughts on paper. Soon, Richard agreed to work in the printing field as a typesetter and press operator for Hyde. He started almost immediately after his arrival in St. Louis and the two agreed to continue their professional relationship after he arrived in the Salt Lake Valley the following year.

As the spring of 1851 began, the increasingly swift current and rising waters of the Mississippi and Missouri Rivers caused the annual breakup of the ice that covered tributaries throughout the long winter months. With adequate water and a river free of ice, the trip from St. Louis to Council Bluffs was resumed and would cover another 500 miles. The journey was scheduled to take a little over one week and the family enjoyed the chance to explore each small city along the way whenever ticketed passengers were allowed to briefly disembark.

With spring, came beautiful greenery, and the return of songbirds along the waterway lifted the family's hearts. As the family neared the last stop before their trip across the plains, they gave thanks for their safe passage up the river. They would probably never travel by boat again.

Once the family arrived in Council Bluffs, after traveling as far up the Mississippi and Missouri rivers as was possible, they were faced with another trial. Under the direction of the Perpetual Emigration Fund program, they would have to be separated in order to live with other families. They were filled with anxiety upon learning they would each have to work out the details of their own journey across the great plains. Tearful goodbyes took place between the family members before they were separated. It was very taxing on everyone, but they all accepted the "easier said than done" travel plans and relied on the experience of the PEF leadership. Throughout the process, the family kept in contact through the mail, and planned on meeting up in Salt Lake Valley at the completion of their journey.

Once Jean arrived at Council Bluffs, she was able to secure a house to live in. She knew she would again need to find work to secure the final payments for the trek across the plains. Janet, on the other hand, already had the money that was needed and was able to immediately secure passage to the Great Salt Lake valley. Janet felt she could be of more assistance to Jean and her family if she went on ahead of them. Joanna and Richard had plans to follow closely behind Janet. The plan would be to meet Jean and the children the following year.

As a single mother and widow, Jean was a striking example of determination as she focused her sights on joining the Saints in Utah. She, however, was not alone among the ranks of many who gave everything they had to travel west. There would be numerous stories written in the journals of many courageous pioneers who would also brave the arduous course to Salt Lake. All would sacrifice much in order to make the trip. Some would sacrifice everything, even their lives.

It cost about $75 to purchase a quality wagon in 1852. The Schuttler Wagon, built by a German immigrant from Chicago, was preferred among those traveling west because of its sturdy workmanship, and Jean was fortunate enough to obtain one for the trip. This wagon would greatly improve her chances of safe travel across the plains. Jean also needed a team to pull the wagon and helping hands that could make the trip possible. A team of horses would cost nearly $100 and money was growing scarce, but Jean's determination was plentiful. She continued to work and save, until she purchased a reliable team.

At Council Bluffs, the Saints excitedly prepared for the formidable task that lay ahead. Each carefully watched every penny spent and calculated the need for its expenditure, leveraging its strength to the greatest benefit. The shared expectations of such a large and determined group facing the same uncertain future with faith and hope, was invigorating.

Located on the west bank of the Missouri River, the establishment of Winter Quarters was a staging area for pioneers headed to the Salt Lake Valley. The area included all of the smaller communities and Mormon camps that were scattered throughout western Iowa. Early in the 1840s, discussions about its location had been held between church leaders and such disparate groups as local landowners and the Otoe and Omaha Indian tribal leaders. After much debate and close inspection, an area near a proposed ferry site was selected. In September of 1846, 820 lots had been laid out and construction had begun. The conditions at Winter Quarters were difficult, but church leaders tried to provide adequate worship services and civic regulations for the Saints.

As the number of families continued to climb in Council Bluffs and Winter Quarters, the need to provide support for those who did not have adequate personal resources to survive grew. To solve the problem, church leaders directed every laboring man in the church to contribute one tenth of his salary for the benefit of the poor or pay an equivalent amount to their ecclesiastic leader who would determine how to deliver aid to those who were suffering.

With the growing numbers, poverty, sickness and death stalked Winter Quarters and the surrounding sub settlements. Young and old, weak and strong began to succumb to the harsh conditions, the brutal travel and disease. In the summer, death accompanied those who had been stricken with malaria, pneumonia, and tuberculosis. Because of malnutrition, "Black Canker," a spreading gangrenous skin ulcer, and the plague of scurvy sickened and killed many. Church leader, Wilford Woodruff wrote, "I have never seen the Latter-day Saints in any situation where they seemed to be passing through greater tribulations or wearing out faster than at the present time." The new arrivals to Winter Quarters were constantly reminded of the history of that first year in 1846 when over 700 people died in the camps by the end of winter. Their history was not forgotten and instituting temporal and spiritual programs improved the living conditions so much that some people abandoned their decision to travel west and, instead, made the area their home. Jean and her family did not share in that enthusiasm and she continued to work and save in order to join a westward company as soon as possible.

When most of the difficulties involved with establishing the community of Winter Quarters were over, the Saints became more adept at surviving in the new environment. Women often joined together to gather food, quilt, braid straw, knit, wash clothes, read letters, and comb each other's hair. This was a blessing and a relief for Jean who deeply enjoyed the company of the other women. She marveled at their goodness and Jane, now nearly six years old, felt comfortable among them as she watched closely, learning and growing from their example.

Although life at Winter Quarters and the surrounding communities could be difficult, it was also a time of great joy for the Saints. Many lifelong friendships were developed. As people were brought together some relationships developed into marriage. The Church held meetings twice weekly where sermons raised morale, and participants could enjoy the chance to socialize and separate themselves from the unkind labors of simple survival. Little Jane joined her mother in attending meetings in which the trek westward was discussed, and with her brother and sister, she helped as best she could as the family prepared for the upcoming 1,100 miles journey. The travelers learned they would travel alongside the broad and gentle flowing Platte River Valley, and cross more than 600 miles of countryside filled with peril and danger, before reaching Fort Laramie in Wyoming. After a short rest, they would then face another 400 miles along the south side of the Platte River and follow many parts of the famed Oregon Trail until they reached the oasis of Fort Bridger, Wyoming. From there, they would move south on the Donner-Reed Trail into the Salt Lake Valley.

On June 8, 1852, Jean and her children, Georgina, Jane, and John prepared to leave Council Bluffs, Iowa for the Great Salt Lake Valley, also known to them as Zion—the gathering place of the Saints. It would be their last night among the friends they had made under such difficult circumstances. There was sadness but also celebrating. As the last lamp was dimmed that evening, apprehension accompanied the family's nightly prayers. Although Jean desperately needed sleep before the big day, it evaded her.

Chapter Five
One Thousand, One Hundred Miles

Captain Thomas Howell was an experienced frontiersman who believed in preparation and persistence. He had made many long journeys across the plains of America, but never were two trips the same. Before every trip, he would interview the adult members of his company, one by one, to learn about their background, skills, and experiences. He knew many of the people in his care were greenhorns, or inexperienced city slickers, and had never encountered the challenges they would soon face. Church leader, Elder Orson Hyde would be joining the company on this trip.

On the evening before the group was scheduled to depart Winter Quarters, Captain Howell invited the adults of his newly formed company to assemble near his camp. After introducing his co-captains, he said, "We will travel between 10 and 15 miles per day. Some days we will encounter challenges such as rain or wagon failures that will slow us down…" He continued his instructions for thirty minutes describing the pros and cons of westward travel. He included an order instituted by Brigham Young during the 1847 crossing of the plains that read: "At five o'clock in the morning the bugle is to be sounded as a signal for every man to rise and attend prayers before he leaves his wagon. Then the people will engage in cooking, eating, feeding teams, etc. until seven o'clock, at which time the train is to move at the sound of the bugle. Each teamster is to keep beside his team with loaded gun in hand or within easy reach, while the extra men, observing the same rule regarding their weapons, are to walk by the side of the particular wagons to which they belong; and no man may leave his post without the permission of the officers. In case of an attack or any hostile demonstration by Indians, the wagons will travel in double file–the order of encampment to be in a circle, with the mouth of each wagon to be outside, and the horses and cattle tied inside the circle. At half past eight each evening the bugles are to be sounded again, upon which signal all will hold prayers in their wagons and be retired to rest by nine o'clock."

Howell cautioned the travelers about the importance of breaking camp each day on time and keeping up with the wagons that were directly in front of them on their journey. He explained the course of travel would follow the famous Oregon Trail where they could take advantage of known grazing pastures where their animals could feed until they were secured at night. The course would proceed to Fort Laramie and up to Independence Rock, where the company would then change direction back to the southwest and onto Fort Bridger. From Fort Bridger, the company would follow the Rocky Mountains and Donner Trail to Emigration Canyon where they would enter the Great Salt Lake Valley.

Captain Howell was clear and concise in his description of the journey and he tactfully reminded the travelers that once the trek began, there would be only one "captain," and that was Captain Howell. Decisions made by him were final, and anyone not following his direction would be expelled from the company. The message was clearly understood by the group and Jean felt a greater sense of comfort knowing they had an experienced guide and leader to follow.

Jane was approaching six years old and she would be expected to help seven-year-old Georgina tend her younger brother along the way. Toddler John would spend most of the trek on the seat of the wagon near his mother but, Georgina and Jane both knew they would be walking the 1,100 miles.

As the morning of Wednesday, June 9, 1852 dawned, cheerful voices of laughter and song denoted the beginning of the journey. The air was filled with the noise of creaking wheels and thunderous hooves as the wagon train of nearly 100 teams pulled out of Winter Quarters, headed towards the almost unimaginable destination. As the miles wore on, the laughter faded, and the songs were replaced by panting and heavy breathing. Within a few days of leaving Iowa, the emigrants realized they had grossly overloaded their wagons. The members of the Howell Company, like many before, began the common practice of unloading all unnecessary goods. Some tried to sell items they now considered luxuries to other group members in hopes of recovering their investment. When this prospect was unsuccessful, they had no choice but to lighten the loads by throwing belongings to the side of the trail. The trail became so littered with debris that scavengers would often collect wagonloads of useful supplies that had been discarded.

As the company progressed along their journey, the long hours of walking turned into days and then into weeks. To the fatigued trekkers, the landscape was monotonous: desolate and flat. Every horizon seemed like an eternity away and every footstep produced a hot and dry dusty cloud that swirled around the plodders' legs. When the footsteps of the entire company and their animals were joined together, mile-long dust clouds formed that stole the moisture from the lips and eyes of the travelers and remained a constant irritant.

Along their journey from Winter Quarters, the company was constantly reminded of the dangers posed by Indians. During the first couple of days after leaving Winter Quarters, Indians would approach the pioneer wagons in a friendly manner and beg for food or trinkets. Many of the natives would present a handwritten note to the travelers, inscribed by pioneers who proceeded them across the plains. The notes usually included compliments about the particular Indian and suggested it would be a good gesture to give him a trinket or something to eat. But, as each day passed and the westward trail worsened, the demeanor of the Indians degraded as well. The further from Winter Quarters the group traveled, the more threatening the Indians became.

The wagons passed through Pawnee and Omaha Indian territory after a few weeks of travel out of Iowa. At that time, both Indian groups were very hostile toward the white man and presented a great threat of looting, robbery and assault. Brigham Young had instructed the pioneers to travel in larger caravans in order to minimize the risk of being harassed by the marauders. When night fell, the wagons would be organized in a circle formation to help protect the group from attacks.

The Pawnee were plains Indians who lived along the Platte River. They were easily recognized by the strange method of stiffening their hair with paint and animal fat so that it stood erect with a horn-like curve at the top. The Pawnee called themselves, "Chahiksichahiks," meaning, "men of men," and there were approximately 12,000 living on the plains in 1850. They were different from other Indian tribes living on the plains because their villages tended to be permanent, making it easier for the pioneers to change their course to avoid the majority of them. The Pawnee were a spiritual people who equated the stars with the gods and often allowed the Mormon pioneers to pass by after learning that the companies were a god-fearing and peaceful people.

The Omaha Indians, on the other hand, were more of a woodland tribe. The name, "Omaha," meant, "those going against the wind or current." As a people, they were often in conflict with the Sioux Indians. The Omaha Indians moved their villages about every ten years based on the availability of women, food and supplies, with most males having up to three wives at one time. The men in this tribe wore their hair in a "scalp-lock," with the hair braided and hanging down on each side of their head. Five years earlier, the Omaha tribe had suffered from a plague-like disease that wiped out many of its people. That plague, along with huge losses from tribal warring, had reduced the Omaha numbers from more than 3,000 people to approximately 600 by the time the Howell Company migrated west.

Seeing Indians in the distance was a common occurrence for the wagon company. Often, members of the group would see the natives monitoring the white interlopers' movements while taking a path parallel to their wagons. The Saints would sometimes see Indians who were either embarking on, or returning from the warpath, painted for battle as the warring tribes vied for food, land and dominance. Sometimes the warriors carried poles with scalps of the people they had killed hanging from them. These Indians were intimidating to look at and frightening to many members of the company, especially the children. On more than one occasion, the children overheard and repeated the whispered tales the adults shared of Indian atrocities to scare each other.

One evening, after only a few weeks into their trek, the company was making their usual preparations for a night at camp. As the work proceeded, word began to spread that Indians were close by. A group of men from the company rode out from the safety of the wagons to meet with the bare-chested warriors they had grown to distrust. The members at camp stood motionless, breathless. White-knuckled hands held rifles in the ready position, frozen in place, while fixed eyes watched the two groups as they conversed. The men appeared to huddle together with the Indians. Their hands were motioning and making gestures that were hard to interpret from across the meadow. Some thought the men were explaining their travel route to the Indians while others thought they might be getting angry at each other as they tried to solidify their dominance and position. Suddenly, the discussions ended, and the men of the Thomas Howell Company and the Indian warriors turned their horses toward the circled wagons and slowly approached. Much to the surprise of the company they were chatting and gesturing like newfound friends. In a show of trust and friendship, the men invited the warriors to come into the confines of the wagon's circle. As the chiefs entered into this perceived safe haven, they smiled as they rode past the travelers. Captain Howell met with the visitors for a short time and then called the pioneers together and asked them to quickly organize a choir in order to sing a hymn or two. The visitors were seated in the middle of a large circle of faithful Saints who commenced to sing a song from their hymn book, "O Stop and Tell Me Red Man," written by

William W. Phelps. The Indians seemed particularly rapt. The group sang proudly, beautifully and with conviction to the honored and still-somewhat-feared guests, who seemed swept up in the moment.

1. "O stop and tell me Red Man,
    "Who are ye? Why you roam?
"And how you get your living?
    "Have you no God;—no home?

2. "With stature straight and portly,
    "And deck'd in native pride,
"With feathers, paints and broaches,
    "He willingly replied:—

3. "I once was pleasant Ephraim,
    "When Jacob for me pray'd;
"But oh! how blessings vanish,
    "When man from God has stray'd!

4. "Before your nation knew us,
    "Some thousand moons ago,
"Our fathers fell in darkness,
    "And wander'd to and fro.

5. "And long they've liv'd by hunting,
    "Instead of work and arts,
"And so our race has dwindled
    "To idle Indian hearts.

6. "Yet hope within us lingers,
    "As if the Spirit spoke:—
"He'll come for your redemption,
    "And break your Gentile yoke:

7. "And all your captive brothers,
    "From every clime shall come,
"And quit their savage customs,
    "To live with God at home.

8. "Then joy will fill our bosoms,
    "And blessings crown our days,
"To live in pure religion,
    "And sing our Maker's praise."

When the song ended, everyone seemed pleased at the good spirit that prevailed among the visitors and the pioneers who cautiously welcomed them. Then, at the urging of the other pioneers, John Toone took the lead in singing several more songs. Toone's tenor voice rose high above the wagon tops and into the night sky. As the Indians sat in the center of the circle, one of the pioneer men leaned over and whispered to his wife, "The spirit of God has rested upon them and their murderous spirits seem to have vanished." Although the Saints were essentially singing of a "fallen race," the Indian visitors seemed to sense the kinship that existed between the words of the song and their own heritage. Brother Toone shared his belief that the Indians were once "a white and delightsome people" who were a chosen people of the Lord. With boldness, he explained the Latter-day Saint belief of how Jesus Christ visited the Americas after his crucifixion and taught the ancient people. As the evening came to a close, the company gave the Indians food and presents and asked for permission to cross through their land without harassment. The Indians agreed and then, as quickly as they came, they disappeared into the night. The Saints of the Thomas Howell Company whispered until dawn about the amazing evening they had with the Omaha Indians.

In reality, emigrants in the early 1850's worried more about the Indians than was necessary. Most of the time, the Native Americans' kindness was what most pioneers remembered. The Indians pulled wagons out of sticky mud, rescued drowning emigrants and assisted the pioneers in rounding up their frightened and scattered livestock.

Chapter Six
Day After Day, They Walked

    Unlike the excitement of the evening the Indians came to visit, the days mostly melted together in a routine of walking, cooking, cleaning up, and bedding down at night with prayers. Sunday was an exception. The Sabbath meant a day of rest for the pioneers. The faithful gathered for songs, sermons, prayer and the sacrament. To young Jane, Sunday meetings seemed to drag on too long. She would entertain herself by drawing in the dirt with a stick, and when that got boring, she would smile and make faces at other children in the congregation. The young ones would struggle to keep their giggles quiet as they engaged in their quiet wars of facial expressions, for the losers were the ones to get caught by their parents. As the meetings dragged on, Jane would pester her mother by continually asking, "How much longer?" She was a typical child in a most atypical situation.

Jane's mother, Jean, made many friends on the trail. One such friend was Hannah Davis Huntsman, an Iowan who, with her six children, braved the journey from Winter Quarters to the Great Salt Lake Valley in a homemade wagon with a wooden yolk and linchpin. Jean and Hannah had much in common and the two became very close. From the back of her wagon Hannah hung a bucket of pine tar for use in greasing the rough joints and axles of the craft. The wagon had no brakes and only a small chain to lock its wheels. She would yoke two unbroken steers together to pull her wagon. Three pairs of unbroken cows were also yoked together for better control on the journey. Hannah's 14-year-old son Joseph would drive the livestock while the rest of her children provided whatever help they could. Hannah's husband had migrated to the Salt Lake Valley with an earlier wagon company in order to find a home and establish crops before his family arrived. Similarly, Jean's mother, brother and sister had left Winter Quarters a year earlier while Jean remained behind to raise the money for her own wagon and team.

At times, Jean had moments of self-doubt as she crossed the plains, reflecting on her burden as a single mother. She wondered what it would be like to have her husband John with her on this journey, or perhaps, like Hannah, at least have a husband waiting for her in Salt Lake where they would throw their arms around each other and rejoice at their reunion. Whenever she started thinking about such things, she would quickly shake herself off and get back to the reality of her present situation. Although Jean was without a husband, she had much to be thankful for and she deeply appreciated the fact that she had a wagon that was newer and in better condition than Hannah's. As the wagons bounced along the dusty and muddy trails of the deeply rutted road, the axles would frequently drag and become high centered. Jean had confidence in the sturdy workmanship of her transportation. The wheels on her wagon were made of three different types of wood—hickory for the axles, ash for the spokes and the hubs were made from black or sour gum fir. The front wheels were three and one-half feet high and the rear wheels were five feet high, all wrapped in steel. Her wagon was smaller than most, with a floor that was made of oak. There were end gates at both the front and the back, which made the loading and unloading of cargo much easier. Horseshoe-shaped bows of metal were spaced along the bed and over the front and rear in order to cover the front seat and the back latch of the wagon, providing protection from the rain and snow when covered. Finally, a heavy canvas cloth was stretched and fitted over the metal bands to provide protection from the elements and seal off the wagon's interior. The long wooden tongue of the wagon reached forward and between the team of two oxen that Jean was fortunate enough to own. From the back of the wagon hung buckets and boxes that carried wagon jacks, tar for greasing the wheels and water. Jean and Hannah learned to rely on each other throughout the trip and often laughed at their rugged circumstances when deep down they wanted to cry.

Each day posed challenges for Jean and her children, just as it did for every member of the company. As they walked ten to fifteen miles each day, the children would watch for pieces of wood that could be used for building a fire to cook their evening meal. While it really wasn't different from a heat perspective, mentally, a wood fire was a special treat and the food that was cooked over such a blaze tasted so much better than the alternate and norm—dried oxen or buffalo manure. Admittedly, the latter fuel source seemed to be readily deposited in abundance along their route and fortunately it was odorless when it was burning. But the thought of eating a meal prepared through a process of burning animal waste was a difficult mental picture for even the heartiest of pioneers to get over. In a less practical sense, the manure chips also made for great fun as the children would pick them up and throw them like a kitchen plate across the flat countryside where they seemed to fly forever.

The evening fires that seemed so friendly at dusk, would eventually create flickering, monstrous silhouettes in the dark that seemed to stretch and dance beyond the confines of the wagon circle. Nighttime could be traumatic for the younger children of the company as the darkness moved in to surround the wagon train. At night, visibility beyond the wagons was impossible and the dancing shadows made by the darting flames of the spitting, hissing fires only seemed to illustrate and give legs to every imaginable fear six-year-old Jane could form in her head. As the little girl became more accustomed to nighttime on the plains, she grew to love sitting and relaxing by the quivering flames at the edge of the campfires' glow.

Each of the travelers would be bone tired at the end of the day, yet even the deepest slumbers couldn't ignore the spectacle that thunder and lightning would bring to the American plains. The frightening eruptions of each flash of light, and the anticipated explosion of cracking thunder brought anxious anticipation of where the powerful bolts would strike next. The deafening cracks often caused livestock to stampede and scatter, resulting in many lost hours, and sometimes days, trying to locate and herd the animals.

Stampedes were dangerous and could destroy wagons and injure or kill the pioneers' irreplaceable livestock. Ira Hatch, an earlier traveler, recorded, "In the morning, after the cattle were all yoked and most of them chained together, we had another stampede which was truly awful to behold; cattle rushed from the corral, chained together from two to three, four and five yoked, and were literally piled up in heaps, some with broken legs, some with horns broken off, but none killed; two men badly and two slightly hurt. Through the course of the day, we had some six or eight stampedes, and it was with extreme difficulty that we got them quieted; we then separated them into squads of ten; during the operation I think I saw some of the tracks of the 'big elephant.'"

"The Big Elephant," was a common term used during the mid-19th century referring to a folklore meaning for the culmination of long-held desires. Seeing elephant tracks meant getting closer to the animal or to a realization of a desire. Additionally, it could mean risking all but coming up short, never quite achieving the dream. Still, there is appreciation for the rousing adventure adding vigor, rigor and excitement to a fully inhabited life on the move, content at the journey well-made for the color and drama of the quest, realized or otherwise.

Most of the company spent each day walking, and little Jane was usually barefoot for the journey. At her young age, she was responsible for driving the small herd of family livestock over the rugged landscape, in unbearable heat and freezing cold, over rocks, cactus and sand. Jane didn't know anything different, so the thought of complaining never occurred to her. She did have the shoes that her mother had made out of the discarded coats of soldiers, but her calloused, bare feet seemed capable of the journey and she preferred to save her "shoes" for nicer circumstances or when the weather became so terrible that they were needed to avoid injuries or frostbite. Even the livestock became sore footed as they trudged along mile after mile. The cracked hooves of the cattle could be repaired with tar but the blisters on Jane's feet would require the eventual formation of calluses to minimize the pain.

Like Jane, Georgina shared in the responsibilities along the trail too. Most of her time was spent taking care of John, who was still a toddler. At times she carried him. When she let him walk, she would eventually have to pick him up and then run to catch up with the wagon train. At times, Jane would watch Georgina wrestle with the energetic and mischievous John and think to herself how grateful she was to be chasing cows. When it was her turn to care for John, Jane thought her duties of pursuing and controlling the livestock was much easier than keeping the toddler entertained and moving forward.

The wagon train company continued on its way, day after day, as it paralleled the well-traveled Oregon Trail. The caravan had to cross the Platte River 14 times during the first leg of the overland journey. Each time the group crossed the Platte, they had to prod and push stubborn cattle into the water and then collect them on the other side. All along the way were reminders of the persistent wear and tear of the journey. Jane's friend, seven-year-old Rebecca Estela Moore Tanner recalled, "There were fresh graves all along the way for miles. In one place wolves had dug up a body; it was lying by the side of a grave. The men got their shovels and buried it again."

The company made their first official stop at Fort Kearny in Nebraska. The fort was protected by retired soldiers who managed the facility with as many as 2,000 emigrants passing through in a single day. For those who could afford to purchase goods, it was a place where one could buy food and supplies. The mail service was very reliable at Fort Kearney and many of the pioneer travelers looked forward to the stop in hopes of receiving letters; for Jean, there were none. She did take time to scribble a note to her mother indicating the name of the wagon company she had joined and her anticipated arrival date into Salt Lake.

Fort Kearny had no walled fortifications and the construction was so poor that a snake could have slithered through the walls. One of the emigrants, William Kelley, described the soldiers: "A most un-soldierly looking lot they were, unshaven, unshorn, with patched uniforms and a lounging gate. The privates being more particular in their inquiries after whiskey, for which they offered one dollar the half pint; but we had none to sell them even at that tempting price."

After repairing the wagons, restocking supplies and resting the animals, the Thomas Howell Company was back on the trail heading west. Two weeks had passed since they left Council Bluffs and the journey seemed to be progressing as planned. When it was time to head out, there was a race to see who would take the front positions of the wagon train. No one wanted to be at the back because of the huge clouds of dust created by the hooves, feet, and wagon wheels that beat the ground in front of them. Captain Howell was especially cognizant of the "greenhorns," or the families who had never been in the "wild west." These inexperienced trekkers often bumped other wagons, upset loads and spilled grain across the plains. They tipped their wagons over frequently and many times couldn't get their animals to move in the same direction. For the pioneers, each step was a planned event. Their feet hurt. Their bodies hurt, yet they pushed on. Cholera was a common ailment, but thankfully, no one in Jean's family or within the Thomas Howell Company contracted it.

On July 2, 1852, when the wagon train was about 250 miles into its journey, one of the women in the company, Mrs. Cynthia Butler Osborn, gave birth to her eleventh child. Mrs. Osborn had been in poor health before the trip had begun, but after discussions with her husband and children, she decided she would rather face the hardships of the journey than be separated from her family. The entire company stopped on the day she was giving birth. The day started with optimism as news of the pending birth circulated throughout the company. Then, as quickly as the exciting news spread, it suddenly turned to sadness with the announcement that the child was stillborn. This was the company's first death on the pioneer trail. The new baby would have to be laid in a simple grave on the plains. Mrs. Osborn was terrified that wolves would devour the child's body just as they had witnessed a week earlier. She pleaded with the men to make sure the body was buried deep in the ground and protected from the predatory wolves. "The brethren were very kind to us in this our affliction," her husband David recalled. "There were no boards in all the camps to get to make a coffin, but they took pains to go over to the river and cut and bring cottonwood logs to place over the corpse to prevent the wolves from getting it." The grave was carefully dug and, the logs were covered with dirt. For several weeks after the stillbirth of her child, Mrs. Osborn's health declined until she joined her child as another victim of the trek. Her dying request to her husband was, "Take good care of my little children for I expect they'll have hard times."

During the burial of his wife on the American plains, David Osborn uttered, "Thus terminated the life of my old and worthy companion. A life, which had been checkered with many afflictions, hardships and anxieties… is now where the weary pilgrims are at rest. We lived together 24 years, 2 months and 22 days. During which time she brought me 10 children, 4 boys and 6 girls and justice requires that I should say she was a kind-hearted and affectionate wife and mother; was truthful, industrious, cleanly and strictly virtuous. She received and cherished the first principles of the gospel. Maintained her standing in the church and, I hope, notwithstanding her imperfections, according to the promise I received in my patriarchal blessing, to receive her again in the resurrection of the just." With the help of strangers who had become like family, Mrs. Osborn's body remained behind, buried beneath the grass and sage as her husband, children and pioneer family trudged onward to the Great Salt Lake Valley.

As the company continued along the trail, they came across two landmarks called Courthouse Rock and Jail Rock. These were two natural rock formations that were bigger than any mountain many of the settlers had ever seen. Several members of the party wanted to see the rock formation close up and Captain Howell relented. The wagon train came to a halt, while adults and children made the side trip. The rock formations towered more than 400 feet into the air and stood alone on the flat tundra. One emigrant, Joel Palmer remarked, "viewed from the road, the beholder might easily imagine he was gazing upon some ancient structure of the old world. A nearer approach dispels this illusion and it looks, as it is, rough and unseemly." A few of the pioneers were so enthralled with the formation that they decided to climb to the top and see the view. Jean, with John in arms and Jane and Georgina in tow, joined the group that made its way to the top of the Courthouse Rock. There, they each carved their names in a rock and enjoyed the view of the landscape below.

After more than 500 miles and nearly two months of travel and travail, the wagon train of weary Saints finally arrived at Fort Laramie, Wyoming—a major milestone. Fort Laramie was a military post that marked the gateway to the Rocky Mountains. For the weary travelers it was the first civilized encampment they had seen since leaving Fort Kearny. The fort was not what many of the Saints had expected, however. Relying only on local Indian tribes, primarily the Sioux Indians, to purchase his goods, fur trader William Sublette had built the fortification in the 1830's and originally named it Fort William. By 1849 the fort was purchased by the United States

Army who had been given the responsibility to protect emigrants from the increasingly hostile Sioux. The most important building within the fort, according to the pioneers, was the post office as it often contained their connection to loved ones through letters. Some supplies could be purchased in the fort, but the prices were far too high for most settlers. Fortunately, most of the company had what they needed to complete the journey. In fact, many of the members of the company tried to sell some of the things they had with them. Unfortunately, the trader at the fort was seldom buying. He knew that he could just venture out on the trail near the difficult mountain terrain and pick up the same treasures for free.

Arriving at Fort Laramie was both a relief and a worry. Getting there had required traveling along the north side of the Platte River, among the powerful Sioux Indians. The Sioux warriors numbered in the thousands and were thought to be the most powerful tribe between the Missouri River and the Rocky Mountains. From as far back as 1812, the Sioux numbered approximately 13,000. As the United States government and the tribal leadership continued to negotiate land settlements, the Sioux maintained smaller and smaller portions. They came to realize the government was cheating them, and hostilities sprang up from time to time. As the company traveled through this area of the country, most Sioux were still apprehensive about the white settlers but generally friendly with them, wanting mostly to trade Indian ponies and goods for rifles and other modern inventions. Sadly, from time to time an Indian and white man would cross paths in violence and the stories would be told and retold, often very distant from the truth.

Fort Laramie was surrounded by large walls made from cottonwood logs. The walls were built not necessarily for protection against the Indians but to minimize theft. Since soldiers protected the fort most of the time, many of the Northern Plains Indian tribes avoided attacking such heavily armed locations. After a few days of rest at Fort Laramie, the company hitched up their teams and continued the trek. With each start, the greenhorns were improving, and Captain Howell was heard to say, "These greenhorns are becoming frontiersmen!"

With the Sioux now a memory, the company now looked ahead to a countryside of breathtaking beauty that stretched out before them. There were a few white families and mountain men living in the area who were primarily traders of buckskins and furs. The traders would transport the materials to cities in the east to make coats, robes and other fine apparel.

As the company traveled, they encountered hundreds of bison grazing on the plains. On a few occasions, the men in the company would hunt them. The hunters would have to pursue the herds several miles away from the wagon train to avoid a stampede. Gibson Condie commented, "It was a grand sight to see hundreds of them [buffalo] grassing on the plains. When they run, it made the earth almost tremble before them. We killed a number of them. Generally, we had horsemen to follow them up, they ran so swift. We would follow the horsemen. They would shoot them down. We then would cut the best parts, the hindquarters, and pack it in sacks and carry it for miles until we get to camp. We cut the meat in slices and hung the meat before a slow fire, until it was dry. I was very fond of it when it was cured. It was so sweet I could be eating it all the time."

Jean's family welcomed entrees of buffalo meat since food on the trip was becoming scant. While most of the pioneers had adequate food to eat, Jean's children were being rationed because of the family's financial situation. Only one handful of corn meal was allowed each day. The various methods of eating the corn meal were either consuming it plain, mixed with water, or molded into a small cake and cooked. When circumstances permitted, Jean would cook the corn meal in the same water she had previously used to boil a buffalo hide; the mixture seemed to give the family more strength.

After many more days of travel, the company accomplished another great milestone when they reached the Green River. Crossing the river in the autumn was fortunate because the river was at its lowest level. Each wagon successfully made its way over the river without any trouble and pushed on to the famed Fort Bridger. When the pioneers arrived at the fort, they were surprised that there were no soldiers, only the legendary trader, trapper and mountain man, Jim Bridger himself. Bridger was one of the most well-known names in trapping and guiding. He was a rugged mountain man who had spent more than twenty years combing the hills and valleys of the western frontier. Many tall tales were built around Bridger's ability to survive in the coldest of winters and under the fiercest of conditions. He was comfortable with the Indians and had even married and buried three Indian wives during his life. When this group of settlers met him, he was married to a Shoshone Indian woman—wife number three.

After caring for the livestock and fixing the beleaguered wagons, the members of the company had the privilege of joining Bridger for dinner. Bridger made sure that he spent a few moments with the children of the company who considered him a kind of folk hero. Little Jane was fortunate enough to sit next to the trapper as he told one of his famous tall tales about his discovery of a "peetrified forest" where trees full of "peetrified birds" sang beautiful "peetrified songs." The children were captivated with Bridger who also spoke several foreign languages, including native tribal languages. He included the languages and the names of real or imaginary cohorts into each of his tales.

After dismissing the children, Bridger sat with Captain Howell and his lieutenants who provided him with a report on their travels. In turn, Bridger provided Howell with a report of what the company could expect as they continued the trek into the Great Salt Lake Valley. Bridger wondered aloud why Brigham Young would have chosen such a place for a settlement. He laughed about Young's decision and described the valley as an area where the water was salty and bitter, and the land was dry as a bone. Bridger even teasingly suggested that he would have bought the Salt Lake Valley and tried to sell it to Brigham Young himself if he'd known Young was so foolish. And as they talked, many of the adults in the group heard him say, "If the "Mormons" could raise a bushel of corn in Salt Lake Valley, I will give them a thousand dollars." As the evening wore on, Bridger shared another one of his tall tales. He told a story of being chased for several miles by a band of 100 Cheyenne Indian warriors. After eluding them for a time, he eventually found himself cornered at the end of a box canyon with the hostile pack of Indians closing in on him from every side. At that point in the story, he became deathly quiet and stared at the greenhorns until one of them asked him, "What happened then, Mr. Bridger?" to which he replied, "They kilt me!" With that, Bridger laughed at his own joke and excused himself, bidding the group farewell. As he walked away, he stopped and turned to the travelers saying, "The Indians around Fort Bridger are a peaceful bunch. Feel free to trade with them. They have quality buckskins and ponies, and they'll help you with anything you need."

The next morning, as the band of pioneers prepared to leave Fort Bridger, some took advantage of the information and stocked up on supplies, preparatory for the final leg of their trek toward the Salt Lake Valley. As the group loaded their wagons and began exiting the fort, Hannah Davis Huntsman noticed a man on a horse riding quickly toward the company. She studied him for a moment and then with a "whoop and a holler" stood up on the seat of her wagon, waved her arms and yelled to her children, "It's your father." A wonderful reunion took place as Hannah and her children embraced their husband and father who had traveled from Salt Lake City to Fort Bridger in order to meet his family and provide escort through the final stretch of their journey.

The weary, yet somewhat rejuvenated travelers then set out on the final trail to Salt Lake. After crossing the shortest portion of the Bear River, the company turned southward and followed the Donner-Reed trail. The Bear River Valley was inhabited by the Shoshone Indians and was a beautiful and fertile area that provided plenty of water and feed for the livestock. After crossing the Bear River and traveling south in their wagons, the weary pioneers traversed Echo Canyon, named for the echoing effect the towering red rock cliffs on each side of the canyon produced. As they walked along, the children began to shout out to the repeating cliffs. They shouted over and again, laughing at the mysterious voice that echoed back from the cliffs. The adults soon hushed children because they feared the loud noises would scare the livestock. It was here that Captain Howell chose to follow the river westward, rather than taking the proven trail over the Big Mountain. This course would cut many miles off of the trip. Unfortunately, upon reaching the lower Weber River west of Echo Canyon, the group realized that because of the narrow canyon and difficult terrain, along with the terribly swift current of the river, westward travel at that point was impossible. Frustrated, the teams turned around and headed back toward Echo Canyon and a larger canyon that ran southward through the Henefer Valley. On the way back, they passed a peculiar rock formation called, "Gutter Defile," because of the two parallel slabs of rock about 20 feet apart and nearly 200 feet long. The formation looked like a giant playground slide and would later be renamed: "Devil's Slide".

With a few more days of travel climbing a five-mile ascent up Big Mountain situated between Echo Canyon and Salt Lake, the company got their first glimpse of the Great Salt Lake Valley. They were walking the same trail that the Donner-Reed Party had walked in 1846. It was also the trail that the Mormon prophet Brigham Young took into the Great Salt Lake Valley in 1847 declaring, "This is the right place!" With shouts of joy and many tears, the pioneers of the Thomas C.D. Howell Company locked their wagon wheels into place and slid down the steep grade into Emigration Canyon—the portal to the Salt Lake Valley. As they exited the canyon and saw the beautiful view of the Great Salt Lake and its surroundings, they stopped and marveled. And then on bended knees they uttered prayers of thanksgiving. They had completed their journey to Zion.

Gibson Condie, a member of the company later recorded in his journal, "I marveled to myself how the pioneers could find their way across the mountains, making roads, cutting brush and timber, to come to this beautifully valley. Surely the Lord opened their way for them to pass through the chain of mountains and canyons."

Jean and her children were among the first members of the Thomas Howell Company to reach the Salt Lake Valley on September 2, 1852. It would take two additional days of travel before the entire company joined their pioneering companions. Jean, Georgina, Jane and John had successfully made it to their promised land. They had traveled relatively free of sickness and had enjoyed health and strength along the way that was sufficient for the task given them. For them, their prayers were prayers of deep gratitude. They knew they had passed a major test.

Chapter Seven
The Great Salt Lake Valley

Before the dust could settle around the cracked spokes of the wagon wheels, Jean's family was directed by Captain Howell to join the other newly arriving pioneers at the Old Pioneer Fort. Jean snapped and pulled the leather reins through her fingers and directed the very tired team of oxen and horses with firmness and expertise, a skill she hadn't possessed when they left Council Bluffs, Iowa many months earlier. The dirty wagon rattled, creaked and groaned and Jane wondered if it could make it another hundred yards before it fell completely apart. This modern marvel of frontier travel had served the family well. As the group approached the fort, they were surrounded by fellow Saints, both young and old, who welcomed and congratulated the weary travelers on making it safely to Zion. Young Jane felt as if they were royalty in a parade and waived to the children who ran alongside their wagon shouting, "Welcome to Salt Lake!"

In 1847, after arriving in the valley, The Church of Jesus Christ of Latter-day Saints had established Salt Lake as its headquarters and agents of the Perpetual Emigration Fund were on hand to meet the arriving pioneers and help them acclimate into society. While climbing down from the seat of her wagon, Jean was approached by one such agent. She firmly shook his hand and then, without warning, threw her arms around him, thanking him for meeting her there and for the support she felt from him and his counterparts throughout her two-year journey.

While at the Old Pioneer Fort the family rested and received instructions about where they would be living. The church PEF had organized and assigned a home for all arriving emigrants until they could either purchase their own home or the home they had been assigned. Jean and the other adults of the Howell Company met with a myriad of seasoned travelers who were either volunteers or paid staff assigned to help those arriving in the valley with anything they might need. Some called the Old Pioneer Fort the "Western Ellis Island." It was like a lighthouse in the darkest desert and provided a great deal of comfort and security to those who passed through its gates.

Construction on Old Pioneer Fort had begun a week after the first pioneers entered the Great Salt Lake Valley in 1847. Through volunteer labor and donations, the settlers during that time were organized into groups with differing responsibilities such as farming and building. Soon, committees were formed to build a temple in the city's center, lay out a grid of streets and property parcels, develop farming plots of ground and, of course, build a fort to protect those living in Salt Lake and to serve as a receiving location for the pioneers that would follow.

Jean and her family were grateful for this pre-planning and the opportunity they had to rest in the fort for a few days. Between much-needed breaks, Jean and the kids cleaned their clothes and wagon to make themselves more presentable before they arrived at their pre-arranged lodging. Days later, as Jean drove her team and wagon to their new home, she scanned the faces of the people she passed, hoping to see the familiar face of her mother Janet, her brother Richard or her sister Joanna. Six-year-old Jane sat next to her, her bright eyes doing the same.

As the family moved through the crowd, Jean couldn't help but place a hand on her daughter's shoulder. Her young child had successfully traveled across the Atlantic Ocean and the American plains to her final destination, Salt Lake City, her Zion. She hoped Jane's life would reclaim some type of normalcy—for both their sake's. After two years of dodging hurricanes, buffalo stampedes, wolves, lightning storms, and harrowing encounters with Indians, Salt Lake was a welcome reprieve.

It would be seven long weeks before Jean and her children were finally reunited with Janet and Richard. They met on the "temple block," where construction of the Salt Lake Temple was set to begin in the coming months. Jean ran to the open arms of her mother and brother with Georgina, Jane and John in close pursuit. Four-year-old John was less joyful about the reunion, having forgotten Janet and Richard's faces. Over and again, Janet expressed how sorry she was that she did not meet them when they came into Salt Lake Valley, explaining that she never received Jane's letter confirming the name of the company she was traveling with or when she was expected to arrive.

Janet recounted how terrible the voyage from St. Louis and Winter Quarters to Salt Lake was for her, knowing that she was leaving part of her family alone to prepare for their own crossing at a different time. With a smile, she explained that her journey had taken a turn for the better once she arrived in Salt Lake. She had met a man by the name of Joseph Dobson, and after a short courtship, married him on the 30th of August, just three days before Jean and her family arrived in the valley. Janet described each of his children she now shared stewardship over and she explained they were living in a place called Lehi about forty miles south of Salt Lake City. She said Richard would also be living with them for a short time. Jean told her mother that she and her children were living in a very suitable little cabin in Sessions Settlement, to the north. Janet wasn't pleased to learn that they would be more than 40 miles apart but expressed her appreciation that Jean had finally completed her voyage and was settled. Together, they made plans to get the families together in the coming days—regardless of the distance.

While Janet turned her attention to visiting with her grandchildren, Richard and Jean caught up. Jean told Richard about a widower she met in church a few weeks after arriving in the valley. His name was Ira Sterns Hatch and he had come across the plains 1849. She explained that their casual visits had become more serious and they were thinking of getting married. After four years of being alone and taking care of her children, Jean told her brother that she was ready for more. Richard didn't feel he could question Jean's judgment—she was the reason he had joined the church, left Scotland and traveled to America. In fact, he was thrilled for her. Jean expressed her concern for their sister, Joanna, and Richard told her that their sister had secured housing and work with a German family a year earlier in Iowa, but she didn't enjoy their company.

At the time Jean was leaving Winter Quarters, Joanna was supposed to be leaving with a group under the direction of Phineas Young, the brother of Brigham Young. Because of limited money, Richard, Jean and Joanna had each gone their separate ways, hoping that they would eventually "bump" into each other again in Salt Lake City. Jean's arrival solved one more piece of the family puzzle, but Joanna's location would remain unknown for several more months.

Dusting the dirt from his sleeves, Richard recounted his own journey to the Salt Lake Valley with the Henry W. Miller Company that had arrived in the valley just one week after Joanna's arrival. Jean couldn't believe what she was hearing and wondered how they could have been so close to each other and yet so far apart. With the trials of the trip across the plains behind her now, Jean was grateful she had accomplished the feat on her own, it seemed to empower her, and she realized she could now accomplish anything.

Richard chuckled as he told Jean that everyone in the wagon company had made fun of him and called him a circus act as he learned to drive a team of oxen across the plains. He said at one point along the way, everyone in his company had to push all the livestock across the river. He had decided to jump into the river and stand downstream so the cows wouldn't double back on them. Being unaccustomed to rivers, he soon found that he was stuck in the river bottom and sinking. He sunk until the water began pouring into his mouth. Nobody could see he was in trouble because there were so many cows in the river. He said he started praying and grabbed a cow's tail. Kicking and grunting, the cow pulled him to the other side of the river where he coughed up water and eventually caught his breath again. He then got on his knees and thanked the Lord for preserving him from an untimely death.

Richard also shared a very special experience he had in saving the life of the daughter of Orson Hyde. He told Jean that when his company arrived at Devil's Gate near Independence Rock, the three-year old girl and her five-year old sister were playing near a fire where two hams were cooking in a caldron. The little three-year old somehow tripped and fell backwards into the boiling water. Richard ran and snatched the little girl from certain demise. Unfortunately, she was frightfully scalded but with careful nursing and priesthood blessings, she recovered.

Richard recounted a funny experience he had as he arrived in the Great Salt Lake Valley. He said that he noticed their mother waiting on the opposite side of the street for the Orson Hyde Company to arrive. He said she crossed the street and walked right up to him, looked him in the eyes and asked if Richard Bee had been along on this trip? "She was standing next to me and didn't recognize me—I was so deeply covered in dust and dirt. I laughed and spoke and, she immediately fell upon me and could not contain herself. She wept so for joy that we had met again."

Richard also had some important news for Jean. Before he left Winter Quarters, he had met a wonderful girl whose father was the bishop in a town called Kanesville, near Winter Quarters. The two had formed a special relationship, and their friendship grew to attachment. He said he had permission from her father to marry the girl but explained to him that he was not yet ready—that he needed a little more time to become financially prepared. Richard had told her father that he would marry her in Salt Lake City. "And now that I'm here," he said, "Orson Hyde has offered me a printing job at the Desert News where I will start working next week." He then told Jean that he kept checking every wagon company coming into Salt Lake but had not found the girl's name on any arrival list. "She must still be in Iowa," said Richard. "When I write the post office in Iowa though, my letters are never answered." Jean asked Richard for her name. "Susan Palmer," he told her, his voice mixed with love and unease. Jean shifted uncomfortably. She tried her best to delicately explain to him that she had met Susan Palmer, and that she had been persuaded to marry a man in Iowa four months earlier. As Richard's face dropped, Jean quickly told him that the marriage, however, wasn't working out very well and that Susan's new husband wasn't to her liking. Regardless of how hard Jean had tried to soften the blow, Richard was still left devastated. He couldn't believe that he had lost his fiancé to another man. For Richard, that glorious reunion on the temple block had taken a turn for the worse—Susan Palmer was married, and he felt deeply alone.

The family spent the day viewing the temple construction and the newly completed Beehive House, which was built to serve as the offices for the President of the Church and the Governor of the Territory of Deseret, Brigham Young. With hugs and promises to get together soon, the family then went their separate ways.

Richard started working for the Deseret News in Salt Lake City but soon left this employment and moved near his mother Janet where he found employment in Lehi, as a printer and shipper. Printing was starting up in the valley and larger and faster presses were being delivered into the city almost monthly. These presses were often hauled across the same rugged landscape that the pioneers were traveling and would provide the settlers with much desired news and information. The printed word was spreading faster and to more people than ever before. It was a marvelous day and time.

Jean continued to enjoy the company of Mr. Hatch and on November 27th, 1852, just three months after entering the Great Salt

Lake Valley, Jean Bee McKechnie and Ira Stearns Hatch married and settled into their new home a few miles north of Salt Lake City in Sessions Settlement, later to be named Bountiful. Hatch had multiple wives and Jean seemed comfortable with the polygamist lifestyle. Almost instantly, Jane had an extended family, a large one with a surplus of brothers. Mainly, she had a father again, a father who provided for her and her mother as she continued to grow in years and maturity.

Jane blossomed in the crowded family and she enjoyed the opportunity to play with so many other children. With children in the Hatch home now ranging in ages from four to sixteen, there was never a dull moment. Georgina and Jane fit comfortably in the middle of the family makeup while John remained the youngest of the clan. By the close of summer in 1854, Jane reached the age of baptism and was happy to have her stepfather, Ira, perform the ordinance that admitted her formally into the church. Jane was now a member of the same faith that prompted her mother to bring her across the ocean, up the Mississippi and across the plains.

In November of 1856, four years after the devastating news of losing Susan Palmer to another, Richard Bee met and married Mary Matheson in Bountiful, Utah. The Mathesons were neighbors to Jean and Ira Hatch, and Jean was instrumental in arranging the first date between her brother and neighbor. Richard had moved to Bountiful during their courtship and after they were married, they returned to Lehi near Richard's home and work. A year later on October 10, 1857, Mary and Richard became parents of their first child, a daughter but, ten short hours after the birth, the baby died. This devastated the new parents, and unfortunately tragedy continued to stalk them. Following the premature birth, Mary began to have physical complications and, three days later, she also died.

Richard stood somber over the graves of his two lost loves, coming to terms with the loneliness that once again intruded into his life. He returned to Lehi a quiet man and buried himself in his work.

Jane was now eleven years old and was referred to by family members as the "Cow-Herder of Bountiful". Her new stepfather Ira was proud of Jane and her ability to care for the cattle and often complimented her ability to work without much instruction or oversight. She too felt a sense of confidence in her responsibilities with the livestock and loved herding the cattle single-handedly. Whether out of necessity or comfort, Jane was most often found chasing her cows while barefoot. Although her home in Bountiful City provided many comforts that Jane was not previously accustomed to, she preferred to be in the countryside where she enjoyed the morning sunrises and the yipping of the coyotes at night. As often as her mother would allow, Jane would spend time with Ira on the range herding cattle. She was maturing and along the way, developing unmatched horsemanship skills. While on the range with Ira, she began to learn more about the cattle business and the challenges the farmers and ranchers faced in the growing community.

One of Jane's responsibilities on the range was to look for creeks or springs for the cattle. Finding water was always a challenge in the high desert of the Salt Lake Valley. While the winter snowpack would provide water for much of the year, most of it, if not all, was gone by late summer and fall. Discovering and developing springs, rivers, and tributaries that could be dammed and preserved for the long summer months was a priority for the Saints. Digging wells was commonplace and tedious but there was ample water housed below the earth's surface to take care of each family's needs, outside of farming. To satisfy the thirst of their crops, water was delivered from rivers and streams or through an intricate canal system that had been developed throughout the valley. Even in the best of circumstances, problems arose from time to time when one farmer would accuse another of taking his watering day or using more than his share of water. Like many other settlements across the country, water caused as many problems as it solved.

Jane was a young lady unconcerned with these small squabbles and was rather indifferent too them. Oftentimes while the adults were arguing, she would sneak away to the western desert for some peace and quiet. It was one of her favorite places during the winter months, for the snow remained on the mountaintops and along the foothills of the valley, offering cool temperatures that seemed to extend the fall season. Utah offered high alpine vistas where the pine trees and quaking aspen created beautiful scenery and cool temperatures. The mountains to the east of the Salt Lake Valley were abundant with wildlife, and deer, elk and grouse were relied on to supplement the increasing food demand placed on the settlers' crops and cattle. To the west of the valley, the glorious sunsets of orange and pink were unmatched as the evening sun slowly descended below the horizon of the Great Salt Lake.

Unfortunately, the Great Salt Lake was so brine filled that nothing, short of a small shrimp called "brine shrimp", could survive in it. Over two 250,000 acres of useless water made up the curious lake, and while it was first considered a blight rather than a resource, the Saints soon figured out how to harvest the salt and minerals produced naturally in the lake for the benefit of many industries and uses. To the settlers who traveled to the Great Salt Lake Valley to escape the religious persecution they had fallen victim to in the Midwest and eastern part of America, Utah was truly beginning to feel like Zion. To those who had studied the bible and the life of

Christ, they found a sense of comfort living next to a dead sea that was fed by a river they named, "Jordan." The parallel to the Holy Land seemed more than coincidental to the Saints and settlers.

While the pioneers were adjusting to their new homes and finding success at many crossroads, the United States government was holding closed-door discussions about the power and influence the "Mormons" were gaining. Unaware of the federal position against polygamy in the territory, the locals looked forward with optimism to the newly elected Buchanan administration. Shortly after his inauguration, Democratic U.S. President James Buchanan somehow came to the conclusion that the Utah Territory, the Territory of Deseret, and their charismatic leader Brigham Young, were in open rebellion against the federal government. President Buchanan, acting on misguided information, became concerned about territorial governor Brigham Young's added position as president of The Church of Jesus Christ of Latter-day Saints. Concerns were raised regarding the mixture of politics and religion and whether it threatened the Constitution. To complicate things for both the Church and the Buchanan administration, the practice of polygamy was a source of social and cultural contention, with country-wide concern being expressed about its practice.

Polygamy, or plural marriage, was being practiced among some members of the Church during this period of time. The Saints believed that their inspired leaders had been given direction from God to restore ancient principles practiced in the Old Testament. After careful consideration and prayer, church leaders began authorizing certain members to practice polygamy, but the church membership at large was not given authorization.

During the elections, President Buchanan, a Democrat, had expressed tolerance within the territories to resolve issues such as slavery on a local basis. The issue of plural marriage was considered to be one of those items that would be handled locally. Members within the newly formed Republican Party on the other hand pledged "to prohibit in the territories those twin relics of barbarism: polygamy and slavery."

After the election was over, President Buchanan surprised his fellow Democrats and sided with Congress in minimizing popular sovereignty, which resulted in a 180° change in his position. In response, Brigham Young explained that the current practice of plural marriage was a freedom of religion issue and only a small percentage of the Latter-day Saint faithful were authorized to practice the principle, but his message fell on deaf ears. America was struggling with issues regarding the protection of its citizens, and to most Americans, the practice of polygamy wasn't about biblical beliefs but more about sex between a man and multiple wives. Even though Young argued that the aggressive action of the Congress against plural marriage, and Utah in particular, was the Democrats' way of, "distracting the nation from the ongoing battles over slavery," Buchanan moved swiftly to effect change in Utah. The government also acted swiftly to limit Brigham Young's authority and the Saints felt that they were being condemned with the same distrust that was institutionalized during their previous occupations in Missouri and Illinois. Many years later, the Church would officially abolish the practice of plural marriage.

President Buchanan moved quickly to find a non-Mormon governor for Utah and based on reports he received from his aid, Judge W.W. Drummond, who had been enlisted to evaluate the situation in Utah, Buchanan felt that the "Mormons" might resist the replacement of Governor Young, resulting in mutiny and possible armed conflicts. Suddenly, the comparative frontier bliss gave way, splintered under the heft of what would soon be called, "The Utah War." It seemed that Buchanan was more impressed with Drummond's position as an associate justice of the Utah Territorial Supreme Court than he was with his reputation and morals. Drummond served for three years in the Utah territorial court before resigning because he complained that the Utahns had no respect for the law, outside their church's organization. He concluded his resignation letter by urging the President to appoint a governor who was not a member of the Latter-day Saint church and to send the new governor with enough military support to enforce whatever rules he laid down. Buchanan later learned that Drummond, at the time of his moral attack on Brigham Young and the Latter-day Saint church, had abandoned a wife and family in the east and kept company with a prostitute whom he had brought to Salt Lake from Washington, D.C.

President Buchanan, without solid investigation, canceled the contract for mail service to Utah and ordered an army force of 2500 soldiers to accompany the newly appointed territorial governor, Alfred Cumming, to Salt Lake City. Cumming was a democratic associate of President Buchanan and served as the mayor of Augusta, Georgia. In 1858, Cumming took over as territorial governor, but only after the conflict in Utah had been settled.

Clumsily, the United States government failed to notify Governor Young that he was being replaced by Cumming, and in the absence of formal notification of the administration's intentions, Young and other church leaders interpreted the army's portent as religious persecution. Young declared martial law and deployed the local militia, the Nauvoo Legion, to mobilize and delay the troop progress. News of Governor Young's reaction and the mobilization of the Nauvoo Legion reached Washington and the body of soldiers who had been sent to Utah was strengthened with an additional 3,000 troops that winter. General Albert Sidney Johnston, who had honorably served the United States as an army general, commanded the now-strengthened force of 5,500 soldiers. Having seen extensive combat during his military fighting career, Johnston was considered to be capable of standing up against the Nauvoo Legion.

When Johnston's Army moved closer to Utah, the Saints in the Salt Lake Valley were told to strip their homes of household items and prepare to burn them down in case of an invasion. On March 23rd, 1858, word came from the church authorities for all members of the Church to move southward to Provo, except for those men who had been given the assignment to stay behind and set the city ablaze.

Sadly, the Latter-day Saints were quite accustomed to being driven from their homes. They had been driven from Missouri and Illinois and had hoped the territorial laws in Utah would protect them from ever having to flee again. In a relocation that dwarfed their earlier flights from the hostile states of Missouri and Illinois, approximately 30,000 people moved 50 miles or more to Provo and other towns in central and southern Utah where they remained in shared and improvised housing to await the outcome of the conflict. The Saints "had undergone a long and perilous trek across a continent to carve out of a wilderness, a haven they could once more call home, free from threatening mobs and hostility. Now they must face this dreadful thing again," Ira recorded in his journal. He instructed Jane to herd the cattle some 50 miles southward to the community of Provo, where she was to remain until the conflict was settled. It was quite an undertaking for a girl her age, but Jane proudly accepted the task. She immediately departed on horseback with the dust of the Utah desert kicking up over the backs of her cattle.

As women and children packed up belongings and headed southward, Brigham Young activated and dispatched the Nauvoo Legion to meet Johnston's Army in the narrow confines of Echo Canyon. The Nauvoo Legion consisted of a large group of Latter-day Saint men who had trained and served together as soldiers. Having learned that the army would be coming from the north, down the canyon while under the canopy of darkness, legion commanders strategically placed men on the cliff tops of the canyon walls near the narrowest points along the way. By stratagem and to help keep warm, the men built huge bonfires that they fed continually through the night. Approximately eight men walked around the bonfire nonstop. With dozens of fires burning and the silhouette of soldiers parading past the flames, the army below thought there were tens of thousands of "Mormon" soldiers marching along the ridgeline, and more importantly, that they were gaining military advantage over them. A retreat was ordered by Johnston and later, U.S. Army Captain Stewart Van Vliet stated, "The route through Echo Canyon would be a death trap for a large body of troops."

When scattered reports of the "Utah Expedition" reached the Saints, they feared the worst and prepared for war. Called home from his New York mission to become an eloquent spokesman for the Latter-day Saint cause, Elder John Taylor prepared a memorandum addressed to President Buchanan and the Congress of the United States, which read, in part:

"We appeal to you as American citizens who have been wronged, insulted, abused and persecuted; driven before our relentless foes from city to city—from state to state—until we were finally expelled from the confines of civilization to seek a shelter in a barren, inhospitable clime, amid the wild, savage tribes of the desert plains.

We claim to be a portion of the people, and as such have rights that must be respected, and which we have a right to demand. We claim that in a republican form of government, such as our fathers established, and such as ours still professes to be, the officers are and should be the servants of the people— not their masters, dictators or tyrants. To the numerous charges of our enemies, we plead not guilty, and challenge the world before any just tribunal to the proof… Try on the plaster of friendly intercourse and honorable dealing instead of foul aggression and war.

Treat us as friends—as citizens entitled to and possessing equal rights with our fellows—and not as alien enemies, lest you make us such.

… All we want is the truth and fair play. The administration ha[s] been imposed upon by false, designing men; their acts have been precipitate and hasty, perhaps through lack of due consideration. Please let us know what you want of us before you prepare your halters to hang, or 'apply the knife to cut out the loathsome, disgusting ulcer.' Do you wish us to deny our God and renounce our religion? That we shall not do… Withdraw your troops, give us our constitutional rights and we are at home."

While those in Salt Lake City viewed the positioning of the army as a waste of resources and money, the government saw it as a necessity. A message was sent to Washington indicating that regardless of the number of soldiers that were sent to Utah, the settlers were going to stand together to protect their rights and property. The government was satisfied when the Saints acknowledged they must follow the laws of the land and began a withdrawal. The Saints on the other hand, viewed the reconciliation as providential intervention.

When Alfred Cumming finally arrived in the territory in November 1857 to assume the governorship, additional conflict arose because Brigham Young hadn't been personally contacted regarding the change in command and he refused to relinquish the post until it was properly transferred. The change in leadership didn't officially occur until President Buchanan notified Governor Young in February of 1858 of the intended changes. Brigham Young peacefully surrendered the title of governor and quickly established a comfortable working relationship with his successor, Governor Cumming.

With the change in governor and the improved relations, President Buchanan wrote an Amnesty Offer, which arrived in June of 1858, and in part read:

PROCLAMATION ON
THE REBELLION IN UTAH

"Now, therefore I, James Buchanan, President of the United States of America, have thought proper to issue this, my Proclamation, enjoining upon all public officers in the Territory of Utah to be diligent and faithful, to the full extent of the power, in the execution of the laws; commanding all citizens of the United States in the said Territory to aid and assist the officers in the performance of their duties; offering the inhabitants of Utah, who shall submit to the laws, a free pardon for seditions and treasons heretofore by them committed; warning those who shall persist, after notice of this proclamation, in the present rebellion against the United States, that they must expect no further leniency, but look to be rigorously dealt with according to their deserts; and declaring that the military forces now in Utah, and hereafter to be sent there, will not be withdrawn until the inhabitants of that Territory shall manifest a proper sense of the duty which they owe to this government."

Brigham Young accepted Buchanan's terms and pardon, although he denied Utah ever rebelled against the United States. Johnston's Army, however, stayed in Utah until 1861 when the Civil War called them back from their Camp Floyd garrison, located 40 miles southwest of Salt Lake City. The Utah War became known as "Buchanan's Blunder" throughout the world. It had been the most extensive and expensive military campaign waged on American soil in between the Mexican and Civil Wars. It ultimately pitted nearly one-third of the U.S. Army against what was arguably the nation's largest, most experienced militia. The "war," as the eastern press reported, saw no real casualties, just the burning of three supply trains and the scattering of government cattle. It was, in fact, a costly conflict that was disruptive and unnecessary. Lives were impacted by a lack of communication, which fueled misunderstandings and transformed a simple decision to give the territory a new governor into a comedy of errors with a lurking possibility of bloodshed.

Following the Utah War, Governor Alfred Cumming quietly took a leave of absence from Utah in May 1861 and never returned to the territory or his political office. General Johnston, the commander of Johnston's Army left also. Many people assumed that both Cumming and Johnston were pulled to the South by their family roots and the impact of the Civil War.

When the conflict was over, the settlers returned to their normal lives, but a price had been paid. Once again, the Saints had been threatened and they lost much of their momentum, due largely to the move southward. The settler's livelihood and economic wellbeing was damaged—crops had been ignored and livestock had been thinned and culled. When Jane received the long-awaited message that she could herd her stepfather's cattle back to Bountiful and return to her home, she was jubilant and repeated the 50-mile trek almost immediately.

After the many long weeks of neglect, the crops were in poor condition and harvest time was already upon them. Every member of Jane's family worked tirelessly to salvage what was left of the plants. To make matters worse, the infestation of grasshoppers had damaged much of the crops and many of the insects still remained in the area. It seemed to Jane that beating the flying grasshoppers and crickets had become an annual event. As she worked alongside her family, Jane would reminisce about a story her mother had told her. The "Miracle of Gulls," which reportedly happened in 1848, was a particularly harsh event where millions of crickets and grasshoppers descended upon the settler's crops—consuming them. The settlers tried beating the crickets with shovels but couldn't kill enough of them to stop the devastation. After praying as a community, a huge flock of seagulls flew in and began eating the crickets. The birds flew out toward the Great Salt Lake where they vomited the bugs and returned to the crops, repeating the ritual until all the grasshoppers and crickets were gone. Jane thought it would be nice if thousands of gulls would show up now to help out. None did, and the pioneers beat the grasshoppers and crickets with sticks until their arms and shoulders could bear no more. Their efforts paid off, and once again, the majority of the crops was saved.

As the autumn rolled into winter, word came to the family that Joanna had safely crossed the plains and married a man named George Thomson in Salt Lake City. The entire Bee family had finally completed their journey from Scotland to the "promised land" in the Utah Territory.

Chapter Eight
Jane and Charles

During the winter of 1859, Richard decided to leave the printing and shipping business in Lehi and migrate one hundred miles north of Salt Lake City to Cache County, where he joined a group of settlers who were homesteading the land. He loaded his wagon with all the necessities it could carry and departed Lehi under the power of his two yokes of oxen. Two unruly cows trailed behind as he made his way toward a new life over the northern horizon. His heart still ached at the loss of his wife Mary and their newborn child, just two years earlier.

On the journey, he planned to stop at Jean and Ira's house for a few days. Several weeks later, he still found himself in their company. During his pleasant stay, which lasted into the new year of 1860, he became very close to his 14-year-old niece Georgina. As the weeks passed, he felt a strange stirring in his chest—he was falling in love. Richard was ten years Georgina's senior and her uncle, but in that era, it didn't matter. Before January had ended, Jean and Ira granted permission for the nuptials and actually encouraged the marriage thinking that the union would be good for both Richard and Georgina and would keep Richard from becoming lonely in his new home in Cache Valley.

On February 7th, 1860, Bishop John Stocker of Bountiful pronounced Richard and Georgina, husband and wife. The newlyweds were ecstatic and wasted no time in planning their new home. With heavy hearts, Richard bid Georgina farewell the next morning and left Bountiful, headed north to Cache County. Once there, he obtained land and began planting crops, all the while building a cabin suitable for Georgina to move into. Within a few months, Georgina joined her husband in their new home

Jane celebrated three more birthdays in Bountiful before a relatively unknown politician named Abraham Lincoln became President of the United States on March 4, 1861. The Utah Territory was changing rapidly and during that same period of time, under the direction of Brigham Young, 46 new communities were established—from southern Idaho in the north, to Sanpete County, situated in the middle of Utah. As Young strategically sent church members to settle communities around the Salt Lake valley, the Civil War raged in the East. Much of the country was facing hardship from the depression brought on by the war, but these were years of expansion for the Saints in the Utah Territory. Young knew that his chances of securing greater areas of land for the eventual statehood of Utah was dependent upon establishing organized and thriving settlements in outlying areas. As each new settlement became independent, President Young would reach further into the territory to develop more communities.

As the Civil War raged on, Sunday school teachers in Salt Lake City were taking advantage of current events and teaching that the war was a fulfillment of the prophet Joseph Smith's revelation more than thirty years earlier when he declared, "Verily, thus saith the Lord concerning the wars that will shortly come to pass, beginning at the rebellion of South Carolina." In a later statement made in 1843, Smith had said: "The commencement of the difficulties which will cause much bloodshed previous to the coming of the Son of Man will be in South Carolina. It may probably arise through the slave question."

In July of 1861, the Nauvoo Legion was once again called upon by the federal government to protect the mail service in the area, a move that gave the appearance that the United States and Utah were finally resolving their issues and developing a level of trust with each other. This was a time of rapid change in the territory with John Dawson, Stephen Harding and James Doty each assuming short-lived tenures as Utah's Territorial Governor.

In 1865, President Abraham Lincoln was assassinated, and the Civil War came to an end. Brigham Young applied for statehood and the territory once again experienced disappointment from another national rejection. The United States Army had finally withdrawn its troops from Utah and the federal government was beginning to show more trust in the territorial leadership. Converts to the church continued to come to Salt Lake City and many of the new Saints were happily accepting assignments from the church leadership to establish new communities in the more remote areas of the territory.

In June of 1865, Jane accompanied a young man by the name of Charles E. Walton in attending the funeral of Governor James D.

Doty. Jane's brother Richard had introduced Charles to her a few months earlier and from time to time, the two enjoyed each other's company. Charles had agreed to bring a wagon to the Hatch home to give Jane and her siblings a ride to the memorial service. From that day forward, the two began seeing each other quite regularly, and friendship gave way to stronger feelings.

Although Jane's entire family enjoyed a much better life in Utah than at any time previous, slashes of despair still intruded into their lives. They watched as cholera took the lives of many in the community, including several of Richard and Georgina's young children. Amidst these tragedies, there was an emerging ray of hope as Jane and Charles' relationship continued to blossom. Jane, now 19 years old, envisioned herself as Charles' wife with the two of them quietly raising a family together. Charles was a good man and she had learned through observation that he was reliable and spiritual.

Charles Eugene Walton was born in Pawpaw Grove, Lee County, Illinois on August 24th, 1847. Prior to living in Lee County, the Walton family had resided in Nauvoo, Illinois where they associated with the prophet Joseph Smith, before the government, under the direction of Governor Boggs, forced the exodus of the Saints from Illinois. Charles' father, William, had owned a machine shop in Lee County where he had built threshing machines—portable horse powered machines capable of stripping and cleaning nearly one hundred bushels of wheat per day. In 1851, when Charles was four years old, his father brought the family to Utah as part of the Harry Walton/Garden Grove Wagon Company. They joined 21 other families who pushed and pulled 60 wagons across the plains arriving in Salt Lake on the 24th of September in 1851. Their trip across the poorly chartered terrain of the plains was quite similar to the hardships and pleasures of those who had gone before them except for the added burden of hauling their huge, hand-built threshing machine. The machine was outfitted with heavy-duty wheels that improved the probability of safely crossing holes, rivers or any other obstacle encountered on the trail.

Charles grew up in the Salt Lake Valley and received some education that made him skilled in note taking and mathematics. He developed a personality that others found friendly and hearty. Like Jane, Charles' family eventually settled in Bountiful and it was there that he first became friends with Richard and then the entire Hatch family. Ultimately his focus turned to Jane.

Jane and Charles continued to socialize together and soon their relationship matured. A brief interruption in their courtship occurred during the spring of 1866 when, at age 19, Charles was called by church leaders to take a wagon team to Iowa with a group of men who would act as guides in bringing an abandoned group of immigrants to Salt Lake City. Charles drove a four-mule team more than 1,100 miles back to Nebraska City. After several days of rest, he met the pre-arranged group of immigrants and with the help of other guides, led the newest group of pioneers back to Salt Lake. By October, Charles and his team had conquered the plains a second time and entered the Great Salt Lake Valley. For Charles, this was a special re-entry into the valley because this time he had made the trek as a man. Equally important, he was a guide to many other travelers—a right of distinction that he was reminded of whenever he would cross paths with one of the trekkers he led across the plains.

Charles and Jane missed each other during his overland journey and Jane was waiting at the Old Fort when he led the immigrants into the valley. Soon, the two began to speak seriously about marriage and on February 22nd, 1867, Jane McKechnie, the Scottish-born pioneer woman, became Mrs. Charles Eugene Walton, Sr. The couple was married in the Latter-day Saint Endowment House in Salt Lake City and the marriage was later solemnized in the Logan, Utah Temple. The temple ceremony included a repetitious civil union, but also endowed the couple with blessings and promises they could not otherwise obtain by being married outside the religious edifice. After the ceremony, the couple found a small cabin in Bountiful to debut their new life together. Eleven months later, Jane and Charles became the parents of their first child, a son, Charles Eugene Walton, Jr., born on January 28, 1868. Two more children rounded out the family with the birth of Magnolia Francis Walton on March 1, 1869 and Leona Jane on August 19, 1871.

Shortly after the birth of their second child Magnolia, Jane had a dramatic and spiritual experience. After a very difficult delivery, Jane lay in a comatose state for several days. While in this coma she dreamed that her father, who had died when she was still a young child in Scotland, came to her. Although she was only 18 months old when John died, Jane immediately knew that the visitor was her father. He told her that she was dying from the ordeal of childbirth and that he had come to escort her home to heaven. Jane pleaded with him to allow her to remain on earth long enough to raise her children and, after a lengthy discussion, her father conceded, telling her that he would leave her on earth for a time. He then told her that he would return for her when she was 45 years of age and she would need to accept God's will and leave the earthly existence. Following the dream, Jane awoke from her coma and recounted the story to her husband Charles and many other family members as well. She tried to minimize the visitation, calling it a dream and the imaginations of her fevered condition, yet she recounted it with great detail and knew that it had occurred the way she recalled. Her health gradually improved and she once again became fully engaged in frontier life, only speaking of the experience from time to time

In the spring of 1870, Charles joined a company of ten men and two wagons sent to investigate and survey a new homestead possibility in the Bear River Valley. The dispatched party consisted of William Harrison Walton, Charles Eugene Walton, George Eastman, William T. Reed, William H. Longhurst, Sr., Joseph Reed, Thomas Harrison, Charles Harrison, William Holt and Albert Berry. Upon their arrival in the valley, the men unanimously agreed that the southern end of the basin, surrounded by mountains and encompassing a cool, deep, 12-foot-wide creek was the place they would recommend for a future settlement. These explorers were not the first people to investigate the area. Cattle ranchers were already living to the north in a settlement called Laketown. The new settlers were, however, the first to place a claim on the ground and the first to think that a community could thrive there.

Charles described the land as being surrounded by beautiful mountains covered with quaking aspen and pine trees, beneficial for building cabins, barns and fences. The building scraps could provide enough firewood to heat hundreds of homes through the roughest of winters. Wildlife was in abundance and while the growing season would be slightly shorter in duration, the amount of land that could be given to each homesteader would make up for the difference. The impressive summer and winter rangeland for livestock was perfect since there were hundreds of miles of abundant wild grass. The early scouts to the area called the settlement Ten Mile Creek due to its location 10 miles upstream from the intended Bear River meeting place. The name would later change to Woodruff. Charles and the men scouted the area throughout the summer, all the while planting and nurturing a segment of crops as a test. The men built several shanties that could get a family through the winter if they were asked to return. As the summer came to a close, the men loaded the wagons and traveled home to report their findings to church leaders. The favorable report of Bear River Valley spurred the Church's decision to send a company of families back to the area to secure land as soon as possible.

Charles and Jane's family were among those chosen to return to the Bear River Valley as soon as they could close out their affairs in Bountiful. They were joined in the assignment by the families of Peter Cornia, John Cox, William Stiff, Joseph Tolman, Adniah Tolman, Charles Dean, Aritmus Putnam, William Reed and Richard Warrick. The Waltons were eager to accept the assignment as quickly as possible but refrained from acting immediately. As Charles' return to Bountiful coincided with the harvest, he took advantage of the threshing machine he had brought across the plains to thresh as many fields as he could in order for his family to have the funds necessary to make the move. Before the arrival of the Walton Thresher in Utah, farmers had harvested their grain by hand. There was a great demand for the threshing machine and before long the family decided to build five additional threshers to aid in the demand for agricultural assistance. Three of the machines were kept in Bountiful and two were moved to Richmond in the Cache Valley where Richard was living, about 80 miles north of Salt Lake.

These were Utah's first power machines and although they were horse powered, they were still a mighty advancement over manpower. Each thresher was painted a different color and, each had its own name. Over the next month, Charles worked day and night threshing while Jane prepared the family for their move. When the harvest was complete, Jane and Charles turned their attention to moving to Ten Mile Creek. With just three years of marriage behind them, this would be the first of several moves the family would make, each at the direction of church leaders.

Charles and Richard Bee had once before considered a move to this region because they recognized the opportunity to take ownership of a great deal of affordable land that they could farm. There had been a number of ranchers living in the region for some time and the soil was fertile and suitable for planting, although the growing season was much shorter because of the higher elevation. Charles and Richard also viewed the area as the type of location where someone who owned a threshing machine could get a lot of work from area farmers during the harvest. And of course, they happened to have a state-of-the-art machine. The two had tabled the discussion at the time saying they would consider it when their families were a little older and could be of more help on a larger farm. When this change of residency came as an assignment from the Church, however, it was no longer a topic of discussion but a matter of obedience. Jane and Charles started packing.

By the spring of 1871, the chosen families had successfully moved to Ten Mile Creek after enduring a rather long and cold winter living in wagons and a small shelter. With his family now working alongside him, Charles began construction on a double log home on the northeast corner of Block 11 in Ten Mile Creek. Charles planted a row of native trees along Main Street in front of his home. The other families were busy doing the same, while also planting crops and building fences. By the end of that first year, the group of 10 had grown to 16 people.

There were no public meeting houses built at that time so church meetings were held in the Walton cabin. Their small home also served as the site for local gatherings during those long winter nights when folks would enjoy one another's talents. During the winter of 1872, the town presented a play in the Walton cabin called, "Ten Nights in a Bar Room." A wagon cover was used as a curtain for the show. The play, written by a popular 19th century playwright, Timothy Shay Arthur, was a melodrama demonizing the use of alcohol. The story followed a miller who gave up his business to open a tavern. The narrator of the story visits the tavern from time to time to tell of the abysmal influence alcohol had on the proprietor and the town.

After a very difficult winter, some of the families chose to leave Ten Mile Creek and return to the Salt Lake Valley. The Latter-day Sain history of that time recorded, "Many were discouraged with the prospects of farming and the cold temperatures." History would show that Woodruff averages more than 50 days per year with temperatures below zero. There are many days when Woodruff is the coldest place in Utah.

As winter rolled into spring, the schoolhouse became the first public building to be constructed. The Ten Mile School was a typical frontier schoolhouse in which one teacher taught all the age groups. The Walton children loved attending Sylvannus Putnam's classes where each day was opened with prayer and a salute of the flag. Charles Jr. recorded in his diary, "My two sisters and I started to school in a typical frontier schoolhouse where one teacher held sway over the temporary destinies of all grades and ages. My first teacher was Van Putnam, engaged from the local talent." While the children attended school, the men worked at constructing a few more community buildings, all the time maintaining their crops and caring for their livestock. Soon the town was enjoying the benefits of a meetinghouse and a post office.

As the summer of 1872 wore on, Charles Walton joined the other men of Ten Mile Creek and embarked into the Hilliard Mountains of Wyoming to cut housing timber and firewood. The Hilliard Mountains was a short horseback ride east of Ten Mile Creek, and each day during the summer, the Waltons' oldest son, Charles Jr., otherwise known as Charlie, would ride into the backcountry on horseback where he would deliver milk to the woodcutters. Ten years old at the time, he took great pride in the responsibility and enjoyed the extra money he earned from tips he received from time to time.

One day as Charlie was preparing to head up on the mountain for his daily delivery, nine year-old Magnolia insisted she accompany him. Charlie didn't want, "any ole girl along," but the ancestral Scottish tenacity was as strong in Magnolia as it was in him, and to Charlie's dismay, hers prevailed. Triumphantly, Maggie sat perched behind Charlie on the horse as he trotted along the woodcutter's trail. Off they went with Maggie's head bobbing from side to side in order to see the road ahead, and talking non-stop. The milk cans that hung from both sides of the saddle flopped and clanged as the riders made their way through brush and timber. Unbeknownst to either of them, a forest fire had broken out shortly after they had left that morning and had crossed the trail behind the children, essentially blocking their route home. Jane and toddler Leona waited anxiously in the cabin and prayed that the children would safely reach the woodcutters. Jane knew they would then be out of harm's way until Charles could bring them home safely. When the children noticed the fire behind them, they feared for their mother's safety more than their own. Charlie thought he would be needed at home to help his mother carry furniture and belongings from their cabin to safety. He spun the horse around and headed toward the flames that separated the young riders from their cabin and mother.

As Charlie edged the nervous horse closer to the flames, the smoke grew heavy and ashes began to blow around. Without warning, the wind changed direction and the fire began to burn to the sides and back of the riders, threatening to trap and burn them alive. Charlie loosened the reins and told his sister to put her arms around his waist and hold on tight because, "We're going through the fire and we're going to ride like hell!" he said. With a forceful command that surprised the horse, Charlie dug his spurs into its sides and snapped the reins. The horse instinctively and obediently complied and sprinted forward into the flames.

Charlie was unaware that his father and the other woodcutters had seen the children's predicament and were racing toward them hoping to stop the frightened riders from charging into the flames. The two children rode as fast as their horse would carry them through the searing heat and darting flames. Charles Sr.'s horse bolted and then reared up as he reached the wall of flames. He dismounted his horse and watched in horror as the flames intensified. The all-consuming heat of the blaze stung his face and he agonized over the thought that his son and daughter may have been consumed by the fire. Two excruciating hours later, Charles Sr. made his way to the family's cabin. To his immense relief, he saw young Charlie and Maggie playing in front of the cabin with baby Leona. Except for some burnt hair, the children were fine. Young Charlie was far more concerned about his horse that had suffered burns to its hooves and legs than he was about Maggie and himself. He also apologized for not delivering the milk.

As 1872 came to a close, the community buried a settler named Stephen Summers, who became known as the first person to die in

Ten Mile Creek. Summers was 36 years and 7 months old when he died. The second death occurred one year later on December 11th, 1873, when Ann Preston Longhurst passed away. Life went on for those living in the small community and the months turned into years. The settlers had made Ten Mile Creek a home.

By the close of 1874, Ten Mile Creek had fully organized church programs in the community and the first Sunday School, Relief Society and several youth programs were instituted. Jane Walton was serving as a Sunday School Instructor and Charles Walton Sr. was serving as the vice president of the Young Men's Association. Many in the small community held responsibilities in the church organizations. Church meetings were held, and minutes were recorded. The only report of concern seemed to be one from a Brother Care who stated in the minutes of the Teacher's Meeting on December 18th, 1874, "Some families were not praying, and some sisters complain that their husbands are neglecting their duties." In that same meeting, John Cox, William T. Reed and Samuel Bryson accepted the assignment to be in charge of all the dances the following year. The church records for the Woodruff Ward showed that Magnolia F. Walton was baptized on July 1, 1877.

As the community grew, a decision was made to change the settlement's name to Woodruff, Utah in honor of Wilford Woodruff, who was a leader in the Latter-day Saint Church. Woodruff would later become the fourth president of the Latter-day Saint Church. The Walton family was growing and enjoying Woodruff. In 1879, Jane and Charles celebrated eight years in the Bear River Valley and twelve years of marriage. Their children were happy and responsible. It seemed as though life was finally stabilizing for them as year after year the cycle of planting, tending, harvesting and waiting through the winter months was repeated. The contentment and stability the

Waltons were enjoying, however, would not last. In the autumn of 1879, Charles and Jane received another call from church leaders to take their family and possessions and join a company of saints who were assigned to establish the San Juan Mission, three hundred miles southeast of Salt Lake City in the four corners area of Utah. While deeply loyal to the church, the two were uneasy with this request. The Walton's met with church authorities to discuss their concerns. The Church's response to them was that Brigham Young had long envisioned a group of Saints living in the San Juan Valley.

The San Juan Mission was a long distance away and was known for harboring hostile Indians and law-breaking criminals who were using the remote area to avoid prosecution. The United States government and church leaders had been meeting with the Navajo and Ute Indians. Fortunately, the meetings had resulted in a peace accord wherein the Indians had agreed to not interfere with the Church's effort to settle the area. Jane and Charles were told by church leaders that they had been handpicked for the assignment because of their proven ability to handle the frontier and build new settlements. As evidenced before, Charles and Jane were obedient and accepted the assignment. Once again, they began making plans to leave behind all they had worked so hard to create and begin a new life in an unfamiliar territory.

The Waltons settled their affairs in Woodruff and traded, sold, or donated whatever they could to begin their journey to a new home in a place called the San Juan Valley. Jane and Charles had no idea what lay ahead of them—that this would become an epic excursion that would be recorded in history among the most remarkable feats of the pioneer era.

Chapter Nine
A Warrior is Born

In 1863 a Paiute man and his Mexican wife became the parents of a baby boy they named Deyuckquasuch. The father, "Old Chee," walked outside his teepee on Navajo Mountain with his infant son in his arms and lifted the child high above his head. As Chee held the baby high, he noticed the sun reflecting through his son's mussed hair, making it appear almost green in color. At that moment, Chee changed the boy's name to "Sowagerie", meaning "Green Hair."

Throughout his young life, the boy responded to the name of Sowagerie (some have spelled his name Sagwageri), even though Pahnah, his mother, often referred to him by his given name, "Mapau" or "Deyuckquasuch". For the next ten years, Sowagerie grew up on a Navajo Reservation with his half-brother, "Scotty," his father, his mother, and his father's second wife. The reservation was situated near the San Juan River and the Blue Mountains of the southern territory of Utah. Old Chee resented living with the Navajo people and often spoke of how the Paiutes needed a place of their own. When Sowagerie was about ten years old, the Paiute members of the combined tribe began to slowly separate from the Navajos, and by 1880 they lived completely apart, often finding themselves in skirmishes with their former hosts. After breaking from the Navajos, the Paiute tribe stayed on the north side of the San Juan River while the Navajos remained to the south.

Sowagerie spent most of his time in the mountains south of the Blue Mountains, an area the Paiute called the, "Land of the Mists." He was taught to track and hunt, and he helped his father, from a very young age, provide for his family. While he was accomplished with a bow and arrow, the introduction of firearms into the Native American culture was much more appealing and soon, the boy was learning to shoot a rifle and pistol. Sometime during his teenage years, Sowagerie adopted the white man name of "William Posey." Paiute tradition allowed members of the tribe to adopt the name of white men who passed through their territory if they felt their life was somehow changed for the better because of the short-lived influence of the drifter. Sowergerie had briefly met an impressive cowboy who traveled through the area bearing the name, and soon the teenaged Paiute assumed the same name. The young Paiute had a childhood friend named "Poke," who got his name in a similar manner. Posey had been familiar with the white race from a young age. He envied their comforts and their many possessions. Still, white people were a mystery to Posey and he kept a distance from them throughout much of his teenage years. He followed the counsel of his father to be wary of them. As Posey and his lifelong friend Poke grew in stature, they caught the attention of their tribal leader, Chief Mancos Jim who soon gave the two young men the status of warriors. Under the influence of Chief Mancos Jim, Posey learned to hate the Navajos even more. Bitter resentment for the white man began to grow as well, though he was unsure why.

As William Posey grew into a warrior and leader, many Indians in the area began to cause problems for the white scouts and cowboys who ventured through the San Juan Valley. Knowing that he would soon be sending a group of peacekeepers to establish the San Juan Mission, Brigham Young requested help from the government in dealing with the Indians. To help with this effort, the government sent a contingency from the United States Army to patrol the region and quell any Indian uprisings. Paiute Chief Mancos Jim relied on his lead warriors, Posey and Poke, to peacefully deal with the army patrols who were sent into the area to keep order. Poke and Posey maintained a cordial relationship with the soldiers, until the day Posey noticed the army had hired three Navajo scouts to show the soldiers around the region. Angered over the army's choice of Navajo over Paiute scouts, Poke and Posey formulated a plan to ambush the group and kill them. The two warriors put a deadly plan into motion and rode to a predetermined location where they waited as the Navajo scout and one of the soldiers unsuspectingly approached. Having the element of surprise on their side, the Paiutes startled the soldier and his scout and began shooting. A gun battle ensued and when the initial confrontation ended, the scout and soldier lay wounded on the ground. Another soldier rode up and tried to offer assistance but was killed on the spot. With one man dead, and two lying wounded in the clearing, Posey ordered the release of a pack of "war dogs." The dogs violently attacked and killed the wounded men while Posey and Poke stood watching.

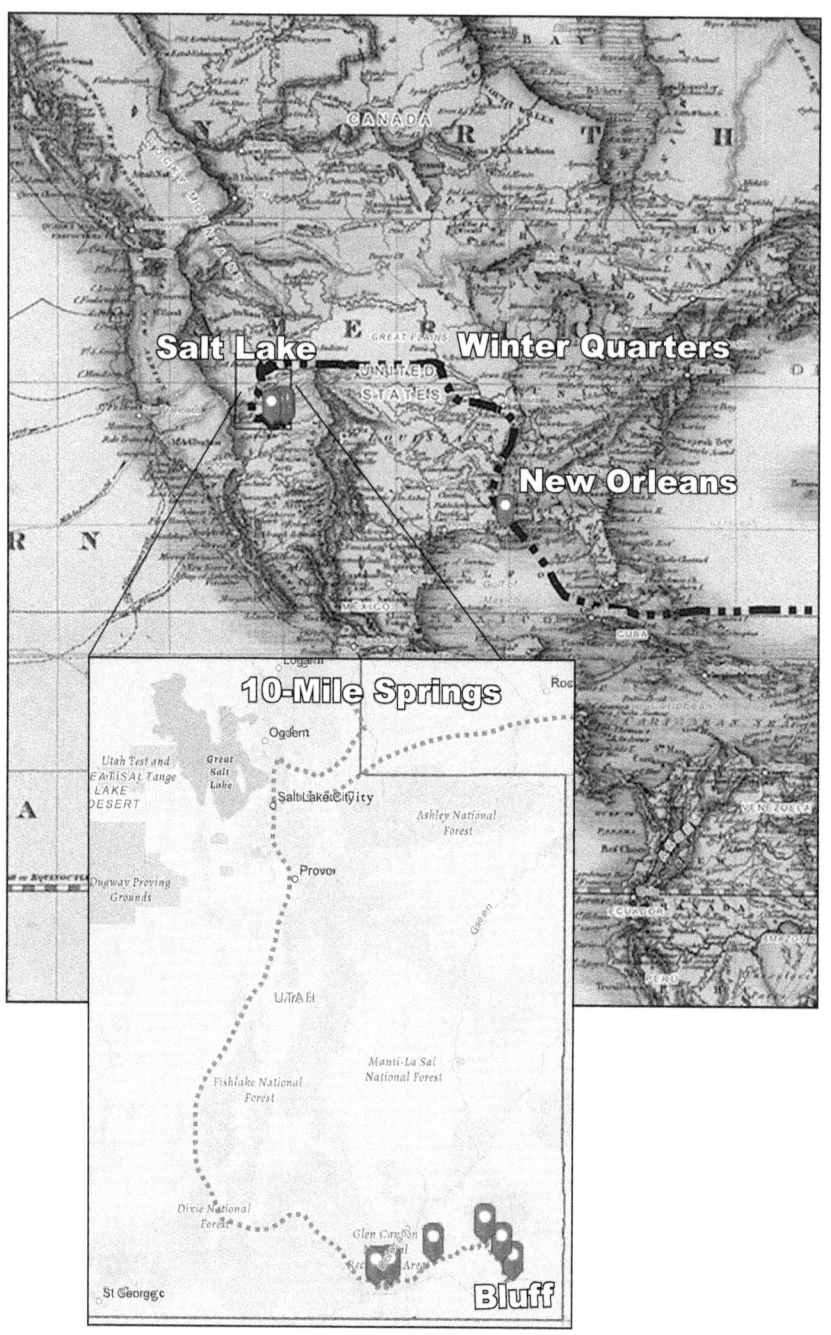

Jane's Travels

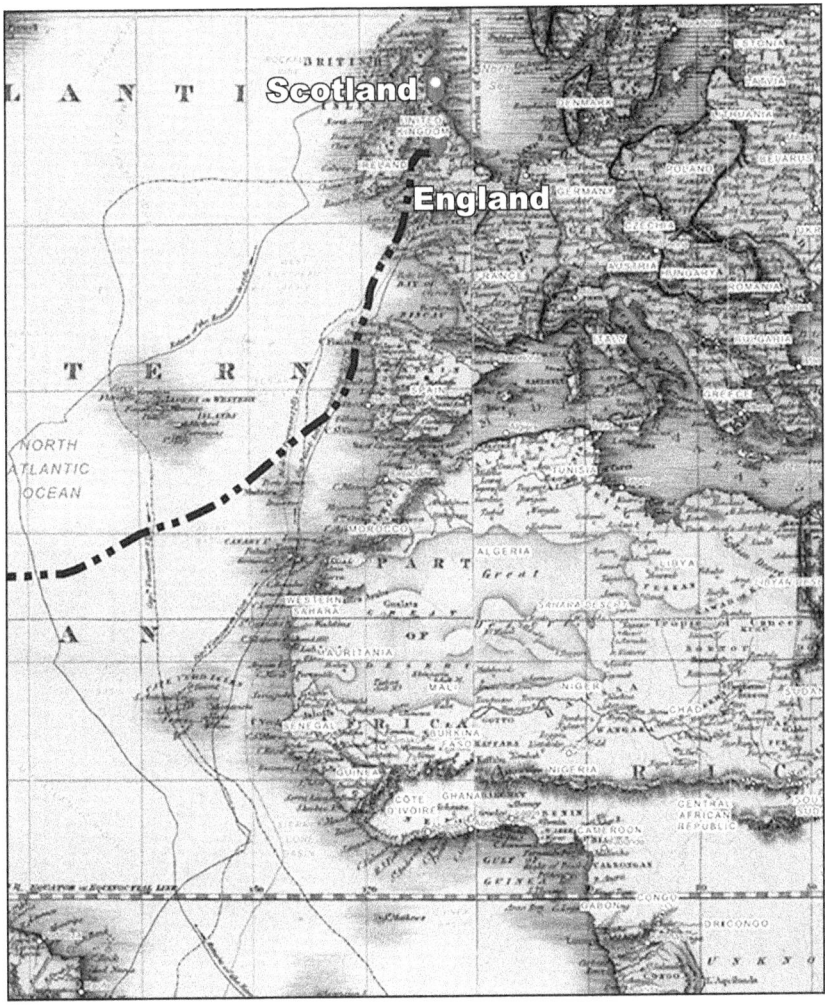

As a child, Jane traveled with her family from Edinburgh, Scotland to Liverpool, England where they boarded the North Atlantic ship. They departed the Waterloo dock for the 11-week journey that would see storms and death at sea. They arrived in America at the New Orleans port where they soon found inland passage up the mighty Mississippi River to St. Louis. From there, they boarded a train to Winters Quarters until they could secure their place in the wagon company heading west to Salt Lake City. Jane walked most of the way and chose to do so barefooted, hoping to save her shoes for nicer things.

Jane's life took her from Salt Lake City, Utah to Bountiful, Utah and then as far north as Ten Mile Springs (Woodruff, Utah). Upon receiving the call to head south, Jane and Charles made their way to Escalante, through Hole in the Rock and into Bluff where they lived until moving to Monticello, Utah.

John McKechnie's Bell at St. Cuthbert's Church • Edinburgh, Scotland. Pictured left to right: John MacDonald (caretaker), Mr. Rankine (Beadle), Mr. Wood (Beadle), Dr. J. MacGregor, Dr. Wallace Williamson. Archibald Ballantine, Mrs. Wallace Williamson, Hippolyte J. Blanc

- Credit: Yerbury Photography, West Lothian

St. Cuthbert's Church

Jane's mother, Jean (Jane) Tinto Bee McKechnie Hatch

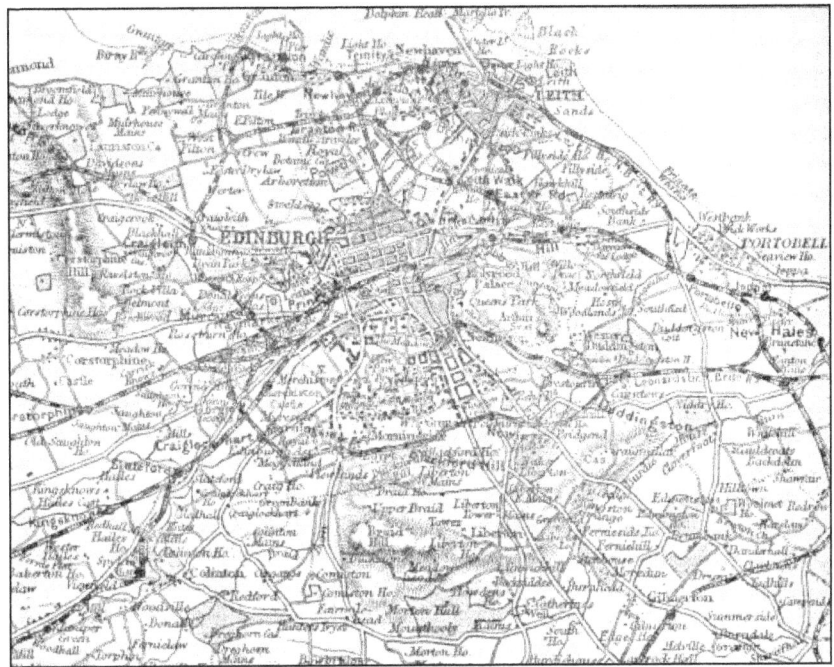

Map of Edinburgh, Scotland and Jane's birthplace.
- Credit: Hipkiss Scanned Old Maps

Richard Moxie Bee and Georgina Bee

"The North Atlantic" steamship. This is the only known image of the ship. The drawing to the right shows similar ships in the Collins Line company (1850-1858).

Immigrant passengers below deck. Source: The Church of Jesus Christ of Latter-day Saints

Right side page: Passenger List from "The North Atlantic" of the Collins Line shipping company. Credit: The Port of New Orleans and Ship's List.
- Credit: Historic New Orleans Collection

Name	Past	Females	E	S	I	Occupation	New Orleans	St Louis	Luggage
John Gordon	46			1		Plumber		1	4 Boxes & 1 Bag of
Isabella do		42	1					1	Apparel
Jane Anderson		45	1					1	3 Boxes of Apparel
Elizabeth do		13	1					1	1 Provision Chest
William Dick	27			1		Labourer		1	
James Wilson	20			1		Collier		1	1 Bag of Bedding
Elizabeth Cunningham		68	1					1	3 Boxes of Apparel
James Goodwin	36			1		Iron founder		1	8 Boxes of Apparel &
Sarah do		42	1					1	Tools, 1 Barrel of Crockery
Sarah ann do		18	1					1	1 Hamper of Clothes
William do	13			1				1	1 Provision Tub
Fredric do	11			1				1	2 Beds
Charles do	9			1				1	
George do	8			1				1	
Henry do	6			1				1	
Henry Lawes	37			1		Blacksmith	1		4 Boxes of Apparel
Jane do		39	1				1		1 Hamper of Clothes
Mary ann do		16	1				1		1 Barrel & 2 Beds
Henry do	12			1			1		
Thomas do	9			1			1		
Benjamin do	3			1			1		
George Gyles	28			1		Brickmaker	1		3 Boxes of Apparel
Mary do		25	1				1		1 Basket of Pots
Thomas Rosbon	27			1		Brickmaker	1		1 Hamper 3 Beds
Elizabeth do			1						
John Patterson	35			1					
Harriet do			1						
Mary do			1						
Sarah do			1						
Elizabeth do			1						
John Hopkins	27			1					
Jane do			1						
Mary do			1						
Thomas Sutcliffe	29			1					
Elizabeth do			1						
Arthur do	3			1					
Catherine Hughes			1						
John Adams	24			1					
John Walker	59			1		Farmer		1	5 Boxes of Apparel
Mary do		58	1					1	1 Provision Chest
Jane do		16	1					1	1 Bundle
Thomas Pigott	27			1		Blacksmith		1	6 Boxes of Apparel
Mary do		21	1					1	1 Bed & 1 Pram, 1 Chair
James Hall	52			1				1	13 Boxes of Apparel
Richd Bell	45			1		Blacksmith		1	3 Bundles of Bedding
Joanna do		21	1					1	1 Provision Chest
Jane McKechnie		23	1					1	3 Beds
Georgianna do		5	1					1	
Jane do		4	1					1	
John do	2			1				1	
William Adams	54			1		Iron Stone Contractor		1	11 Box of Apparel
Jemima do		18	1					1	2 Boxes of Tools
William do	16			1				1	1 Provision Chest
Alexander do	11			1				1	2 Beds & 1 Mattress
Maryanah Thompson		24	1					1	1 Gun
John Thompson	22			1		Carpenter	1		
Isabella Henderson		66	1					1	
Isabella do		16	1					1	
John Marsden	19			1		Gardner		1	4 Boxes of Apparel
John Ufton	20			1		Farmer		1	2 Provision Chests
Robt Ufton	22			1		Farmer		1	3 Boxes of Apparel
Sarah do		18	1					1	1 Gun

LATTER-DAY SAINTS'

MILLENNIAL STAR.

VOLUME XII.

LIVERPOOL:
EDITED AND PUBLISHED BY ORSON PRATT,
15, WILTON STREET, ST. ANNE STREET.

MDCCCL.

ARRIVAL OF THE "NORTH ATLANTIC."—The ship "North Atlantic," which sailed from this port September the 4th, arrived at New Orleans on the 1st day of November. The passage was rather lengthy but safe and pleasant. There were two deaths—Betty Hulme, aged 63, Katren Bonner, aged 3 years. There was one baptized during the voyage, Ann Burton, from Whaploade, Lincolnshire, on the 15th of September. Two infants were born during the voyage.

Notice from the Millennial Star announcing the arrival of the ship, "The North Atlantic" into the Port of New Orleans, Louisiana. On November 1, 1850. The ship sailed with 357 people on board. Elder David Sudworth was the priesthood leader on the ship. This voyage was termed, "The Forty Ninth Company." There was one baptism on board, Ann Burton from Whaploade, Lincolnshire on 15 September 1850. Two deaths were recorded, Betty Hulme (age 63) and Katren Bonner (age 3). Two infants were born during the journey. Source(s): BMR, Book #1043, pp. 59-73 (FHL #025,690); Customs #292 (FHL #200,165).

Captain Henry Cook acknowledges the arrival of the ship North Atlantic into New Orleans. Credit: Historic New Orleans Collection

The New Orleans "The Daily Crescent" contained the information on arriving and departing sea journeys as well as Mississippi River trips.
(Historic New Orleans Collection)

November 2, 1850 Advertisements in "The Daily Crescent" showing the names of the steamships leaving New Orleans for travel up the Mississippi River to St. Louis.

This is where Jane's family secured passage on the steamship "Pacific" which was piloted by Captain Fithian.
Credit: Historic New Orleans Collection

The "Pacific" was also owned by the Collins Line. This is believed to be the steamship Jane and her family secured for the trip up the Mississippi River, leaving New Orleans on November 2, 1850. Credit: Historic New Orleans Collection

Digital ID: cph 3a09862 Reproduction Number: LC-USZ62-7210 (b&w film copy neg.) Repository: Library of Congress Prints and Photographs Division, Washington, DC 20540 USA

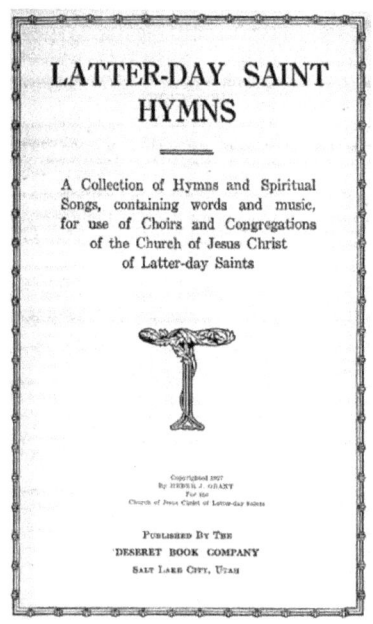

When approached by Native Americans along their journey, the saints would commence to singing a song from their hymn book, "O Stop and Tell Me Red Man," written by William W. Phelps.

No. 64. O Stop and Tell Me, Red Man.

William W. Phelps. (7's & 6's.)

1. O stop and tell me, Red Man, Who are you, why you roam,
And how you get your living; Have you no God, no home?
With stature straight and portly, And decked in native pride,
With feathers, paints and brooches, He willingly replied:

2. "I once was pleasant Ephraim, When Jacob for me prayed;
But oh, how blessings vanish, When man from God has strayed!
Before your nation knew us, Some thousand moons ago,
Our fathers fell in darkness, And wandered to and fro.

3. "And long they've lived by hunting Instead of works and arts,
And so our race has dwindled To idle Indian hearts.
Yet hope within us lingers, As if the Spirit spoke,
He'll come for your redemption, And break the Gentile yoke.

4. "And all your captive brothers From ev'ry clime shall come,
And quit their savage customs, To live with God at home.
Then joy will fill your bosoms, And blessings crown our days,
To live in pure religion, And sing our Maker's praise."

Fort Bridger 1851. Photo in family history records and taken by an unknown source.

Echo Canyon, Utah named for how the voices would echo off the canyon walls. Credit: Mike King, 2020

Pioneers entering Salt Lake Valley 5-years before Jane's Party. Uknown source

Jane McKechnie Walton   Charles Eugene Walton

This is the Walton Blacksmith Shop. It is unknown if this was built before the Walton's crossed the plains or after. Photograph from unknown source, family history.

The Waltons built their home in the northeast corner of Block 11. Block 11 is located at 100 South (one block south of the Monte Cristo Road) and Main Street.

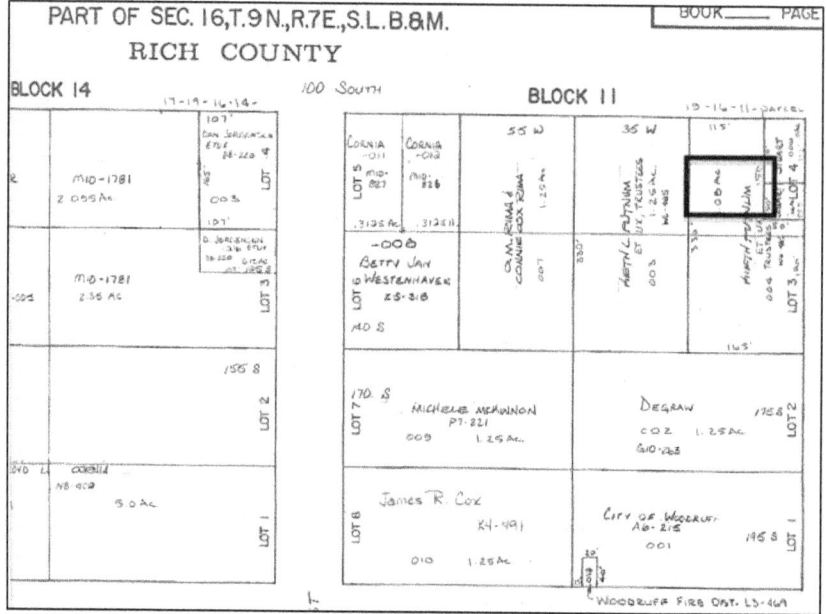

The Walton cabin would have stood where the black box is on the northeast corner of Block 11. Parts of the rock foundation were still here in 1960.

Below is an original cabin from the Walton era. Credit: Mike King

For many years, the Walton Thresher was still in use. This one was updated with a steam engine to power it. Photograph courtesy of Walton Family History. Note: This photograph is also in the publication, "The First 100 Years in Woodruff" but is marked indicating that this thresher is the Neville Thresher. All we know for sure is that both the Neville's and the Walton's were early settlers of Woodruff.

Below: Neville Blacksmith Shop in 1870s from "The First 100 Years in Woodruff" Credit:Judy Stuart, Woodruff, Utah Historian.

Paiute Chief Mancos Jim

Credit: Dr. Trevor Curb and Dr. Steve Lacy, *Footprints from the Past, Inc.* Copyright 1979

Dance Hall Rock on the trail to Hole in the Rock. Credit: Mike King, 2019

The Hole in the Rock trail. This 60-mile route is covered in sandstone and rock. Credit: Mike King, 2019

Below: Hole in the Rock route. Map discovered in Walton Family History - source unknown.

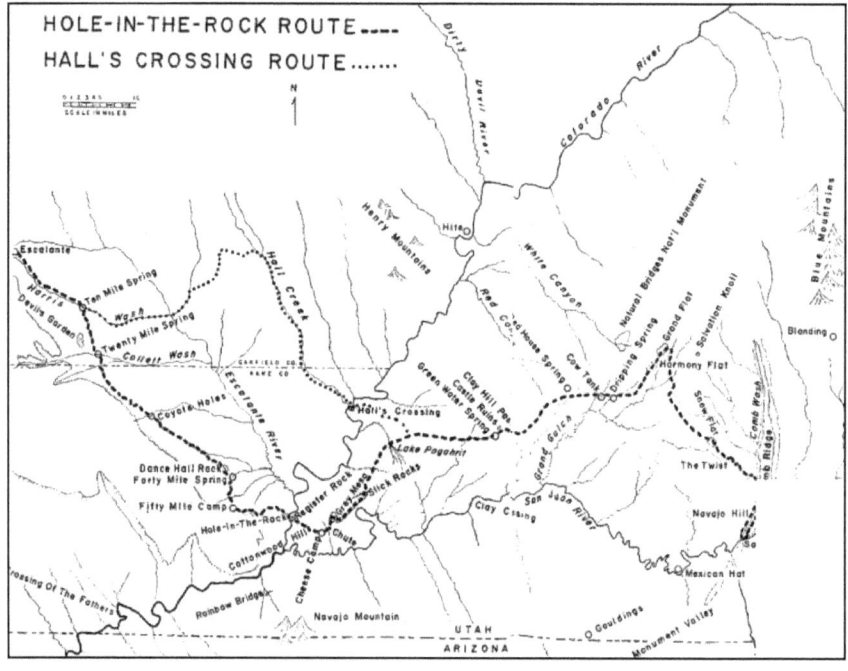

Rendering of what the Hole-in-the-Rock looked like when discovered, a "3-foot gap that a man could barely fit through." Credit: Mike King, 2009

Below: How the "Hole" looks today after pioneers blasted and chipped the rock away leaving a entrance wide enough for a wagon to squeeze through.

The Colorado River now covers the bottom of the canyon which was nearly 2,000 feet down.

The photograph to the left shows how steep the grade was for the first 700 feet. Credit: Mike King, 2009

"Uncle Ben's Dugway" shows holes that were drilled into mountainside to place poles so that the wagons could move down the mountain.
Credit: Bureau of Reclamation

Below: One of the original wagons taken through Hole in the Rock. Now stored at the Bluff Historical Society in Bluff, Utah. Credit: Mike King, 2009

One of the original Bluff homes, restored in its original position by the Bluff Historical Society. Credit: Mike King, 2009

Bluff School. (Courtesy of Dr. Trevor Curb and Dr. Steve Lacy, Footprints from the Past, Inc. Copyright 1979) Note: A copy of this photo is in the Bluff Historical Center indicating this is an early Bluff home.

Children on a Sunday School outing of the Bluff Ward.
Credit: Bluff Historical Society and Charles Goodman.

Bluff Meetinghouse Restored. Credit: Bluff Historical Society.
Credit: Mike King, 2009

Jane's sister Georgina and mother Jean.
Credit: RJM Bee Family

Kumen Jones house was one of the first rock homes built in Bluff. Built in 1880. Credit: Bluff Historical Society.

San Juan Co-Operative Store. Organized on April 24, 1882 with Charles Walton Sr. serving as one of the Directors. The business was later incorporated in 1886.

"The Old Swing Tree in Bluff..." A fenced lane, bordered by poplar trees, wild rose bushes, wild plum trees & strawberry bushes led to the river and the nostalgic swing.

The tree was swept away in the floods on 1908.
Credit: Bluff Historical Society.

The Navajo Twins in Bluff, Utah. Credit: Mike King, 2009

View looking from Bluff Fort. Credit: Mike King, 2009

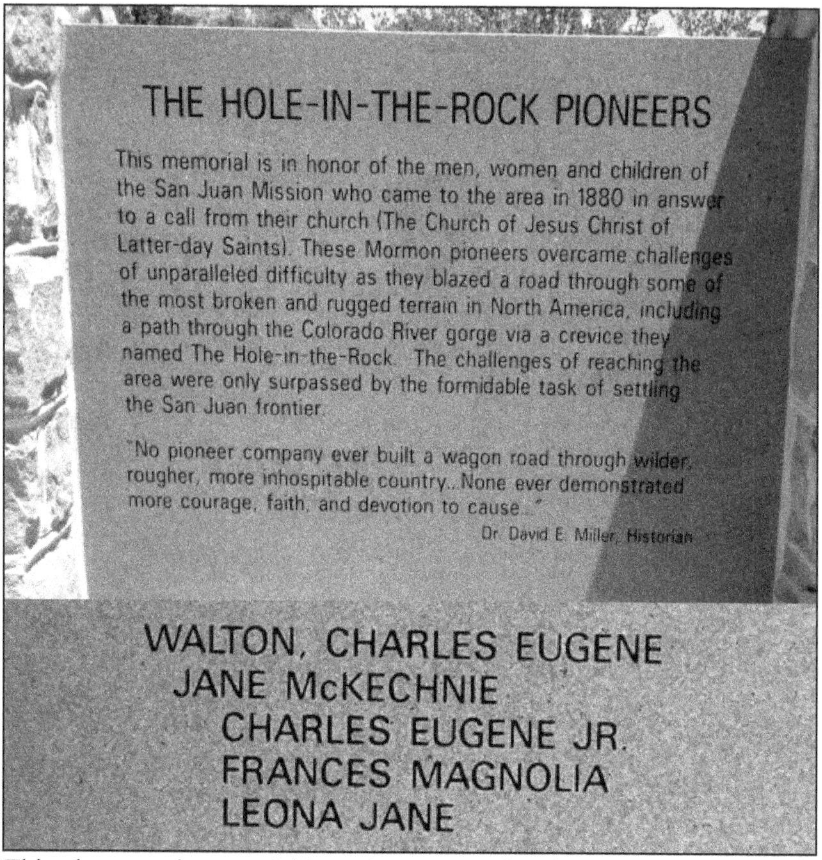

THE HOLE-IN-THE-ROCK PIONEERS

This memorial is in honor of the men, women and children of the San Juan Mission who came to the area in 1880 in answer to a call from their church (The Church of Jesus Christ of Latter-day Saints). These Mormon pioneers overcame challenges of unparalleled difficulty as they blazed a road through some of the most broken and rugged terrain in North America, including a path through the Colorado River gorge via a crevice they named The Hole-in-the-Rock. The challenges of reaching the area were only surpassed by the formidable task of settling the San Juan frontier.

"No pioneer company ever built a wagon road through wilder, rougher, more inhospitable country...None ever demonstrated more courage, faith, and devotion to cause."

Dr. David E. Miller, Historian

WALTON, CHARLES EUGENE
JANE McKECHNIE
CHARLES EUGENE JR.
FRANCES MAGNOLIA
LEONA JANE

This plaque and memorial have been erected at the Bluff Historical site. Credit: Mike King, 2009

Below: Original pioneer cabin in Bluff, Utah at the Bluff Historical site. Credit: Mike King, 2009

Chief William Posey, (Courtesy of Dr. Trevor Curb and Dr. Steve Lacy, *Footprints from the Past, Inc.* Copyright 1979)

Back L-R: Tom Evans, John Rogerson, Charles Walton, Wilford Christensen
From L-R: Fletcher Bronson, S.T. Hibbs, Bishop F.I. Jones, Leo Butt. Source: Walton Family History

Below: Jane McKechnie Walton and Charles E. Walton (arrows) after church at the Old School House - Bluff in 1888. Source: Walton Family History

Monticello, Utah in the late 1890s. House in top left hand corner is the first brick schoolhouse. Top center is the Log Church and the Farmer's Exchange Store is in the top right portion of the photograph. A typical home is shown bottom left of the photo which was found in the Walton Family History.

Below: The Walton family home in the 1890s about the time Jane died.
Source: Walton Family History

Original period home at 100 S 200 E in Monticello, Utah as it would have looked then. (inset is actual home today with additions) Photo manipulated by Mike King, 2009

The Walton family Springfield 45-70 rifle. Photo from the Walton Family History - source: unknown.

Newspaper article from the Ogden Standard Examiner showing Tom Roach arrest in Ogden, Utah (325 miles away) on November 25, 1890.

Police Court News.

Business in the police court was very dull yesterday. Monday is usually a busy day, but yesterday was an exception to the rule, only two cases appearing before his honor.

Tom Roach, convicted of drunkenness was fined $5 including costs.

Ed Irwin, charged with the same offence, donated $5 and costs to the City for his folly.

Original San Juan County Court docket entry to reissue the warrant for the arrest of Tom Roach for murder. Proof that Tom Roach wasn't apprehended by Butt or reported captured by Chief Posey and his warriors as of June 15, 1896. Source: San Juan County Court. Monticello, Utah

Sheriff Willard (Dick) George Butt. Credit: San Juan County Sheriff's Office, Utah

Old Log Church in Monticello, Utah where Jane was shot and killed. Built in 1888 for religious activities. It was also used for community events, as a school and a refuge for the homeless. Credit: The Historical Marker Database.

Jane (seated) and her sister Georgina. There is considerable controversy over which one is Jane. Some Walton family members insist it is the standing woman. Research and images at the Bluff Fort support that the accurate image of Jane is as stated above.
Credit: San Juan Historical Commission 21558 and donor Harold R. Allen.

Above: Jane's daughter Magnolia and husband John Ezra Bailey.

Left: Jane's son Charles Walton Jr. and wife Emma with my grandfather, Clifford Walton Bailey

Left: Charles Walton Sr. shortly before his death. Below: The survivors of Hole in the Rock meet for the last time.

Chapter Ten
Plenty of "Stickie-ta-gudy"

At the annual conference of the Church of Jesus Christ of Latter-day Saints, held in the Bear River Valley, Charles and Jane's names were announced as part of a group of Saints who had been selected by the Church's First Presidency to settle the San Juan River region of the Utah Territory. Several days earlier, the Walton's had had a personal visit from several members of the Church's Quorum of the Twelve Apostles extending the call to go south. The couple had accepted the call and knew that the announcement would come in the meeting. The Walton's, however, were surprised to learn that they were the only family traveling from the northern reaches of the territory. This meant that they had several more weeks of travel, and more importantly, a shorter amount of time to prepare to leave their home and friends. Church leaders asked Charles to act as a scribe for the newly formed expedition made up, primarily, of settlers who were coming from the central and southern areas of the Utah territory. Charles and Jane assumed their call was based on their history of homesteading new frontiers in Bountiful and Ten Mile Creek.

When the conference ended, Jane and Charles still had many questions that needed answering. They wondered what would happen to their crops and home and how they would cover the expenses for the trip. They were informed that the Church would pay for their expenses, and their crops and property would become part of the church owned Bishop's Storehouse. The Bishop's Storehouse was a humanitarian effort to store supplies and resources that could be used in times of need. The Waltons were promised that they would have all of the provisions needed to travel to San Juan and establish a community.

The apostles reiterated President Brigham Young's strong desire to settle the southern region of the territory. They said that for many years President Young had wanted to occupy the area, but placed the decision "on hold" several times, primarily because of the unrest with the Indians. The Navajo and Ute Indians had been troublesome, and they were conducting raids on the early inhabitants of the region, stealing their horses and property and creating general unrest. In addition to the Indian problems, the region had become a haven for outlaw cowboys who were evading the law. In short, the region was relatively unsafe. The Waltons were also told that the group they would be joining had also been "handpicked" for the assignment in an effort to establish harmony between the Indian tribes and the newly arriving white settlers. Charles and Jane had already proven their ability to settle in hostile and unforgiving areas, and while they may not have looked forward to the new adventure, they had accepted the call, believing it had come from church leaders who acted on inspiration from God. Elder Erastus Snow of the Church's leadership explained that the United States government and church officials had been struggling to promote peace with the Indians in the San Juan River region, but the raids, threats and assaults had failed to stop. He went on to say church leaders had finally invited the Navajo tribal chief to come to Salt Lake City to discuss a peaceful negotiation. Thankfully, the meetings had ended successfully with the Indian returning to the San Juan area with an armload of presents from their new associates as well as an agreement to stop molesting the settlers. Regrettably, soon after the meeting and the chief's return home, three Navajo men were killed in an area called Ranch Valley. The Navajo were convinced they had been double-crossed by the Latter-day Saints and vowed a war to the finish. Snow explained that the Church had sent a contingency of men to meet with the Navajo leaders, this time on their land, not in Salt Lake City. After lengthy negotiations, peace had again been restored to the region. Snow reassured the Waltons by telling them the Church did not want to place their family and the other settlers in harm's way and they were promised that the call to settle the San Juan came after a great deal of fasting and prayer. The settlers had been carefully selected to promote peace and friendship and were promised they would be protected in the journey. Over the next 30 days the Walton family began dispersing their assets to the remaining members of Woodruff.

As September dissolved into early October, Jane and Charles spent the days packing their wagon and tying up loose ends. They frantically loaded the last few personal items into the tiny vacant spaces in and around their wagon and the excitement of the new adventure began to peak. The work of loading was done, and the family was ready for their new adventure. Most of Woodruff's residents turned out to say goodbye to the Waltons, bringing baskets of food for their first length of the journey to Bountiful. On October 2nd, 1879, after asking for providential guidance, Charles snapped the reins of the heavily loaded wagon and the family was on their way. According to the expert guides who laid out the San Juan expedition, the trek would take about 6 weeks to travel the 400 miles from Woodruff to the final destination.

Eleven-year-old Charlie, with the help of 10 year-old Maggie, kept the 30 head of livestock, a yoke of wild bulls, and a yoke of wild steers moving with the wagon that was pulled by the Walton's four horses. Eight-year-old Leona rode in the wagon and would jump off from time to time to help push along any wayward animals. Three miles into the trip a chain broke on the wagon and damaged part of the "reach" which held the harness in place. Thinking it was as good a place as any to eat some of the food they had been given, the Walton's relaxed by a stream as Charles repaired the wagon. It wasn't long before they were back on the trail and lumbering toward the Great Salt Lake Valley. The family traveled nearly twenty-two miles that first day and after narrowly escaping a few "tip overs" they camped for the night. During the first few days of travel, they endured thunderstorms, fought swollen rivers and experienced equipment failures. Happily, they pulled into Bountiful on October 8th where they stayed a few days with Jean and Ira Hatch. It was a welcomed reunion.

While in Bountiful, Charles and Jane drove their wagon to Salt Lake City where they met with several church leaders including Elder Erastus Snow and the newly called president of the San Juan Mission, Silas Smith. They were given additional supplies and items intended for the mission. The Waltons insisted on paying for most of the items from their own cash reserves. Their intended short stay in Bountiful extended into two weeks and on October 17th they once again loaded their wagon and headed south toward Escalante, Utah where they would rendezvous with the other members of the expedition at a rock formation called "Dance Hall Rock." From there, the entire group would travel together to the south and east, into the four corners of the San Juan region. The group would rely on maps created by scouts who supposedly had previous knowledge of the area.

Those scouts had also determined that the route was not only the fastest, but the safest from Indian attack. After convincing both the United States government and church leaders of the scout's opinion, the decision was made to follow the route and to ensure success. A member of the original scouting team joined the members of the expedition. The Waltons and every member of the mission looked forward to the meeting at Dance Hall Rock and the Colorado River with great anticipation.

The distance from Bountiful to Escalante, Utah was approximately three hundred miles and required traveling over desert terrain and through several mountain ranges. The journey proved to be more difficult than Charles had initially been told and the slow pace the trekkers were forced to take caused him to get frustrated. He worried about inconveniencing the other travelers who were waiting at Dance Hall Rock. They pushed on through the rugged mountain terrain and arrived in Marysvale, Utah, still more than one hundred miles from the meeting site. The journey had been relatively uneventful until the group reached the Escalante region, where the dirt trails turned to solid rock. The teams of horses began to struggle as they pulled the loads. The horses tried to dig their hooves into the unforgiving stone but slipped with every step. The rocky conditions not only caused damage to the horses' hooves, but to the wagons as well as they jolted to and fro with every foot of progress. A grueling week later, the Waltons pulled into the Escalante Valley and made their way through the desert soil to the meeting spot, Dance Hall Rock. The gigantic rock formation resembled an amphitheater with a flat rock floor and a backdrop of arching red rock. It was a perfect setting for music and dancing.

Since the Waltons were late arriving, other members of the group had scouted ahead. After the initial greetings, Charles met with Platt D. Lyman, who told him that the desert between Dance Hall Rock and another landmark called Hole in the Rock, was the worst country he'd ever seen. Hole in the Rock was the name the scouts had given an opening in the cliffs overlooking the Colorado River. The group had planned to set camp near the landmark and then make their way down the cliffs through the opening to the riverbank. They would then transit across the river, preparatory to their final descent into the San Juan valley. To Charles's astonishment, he was told that the "hole" was actually a small, 3-foot-wide crevice that sliced through the canyon wall. The opening would only allow for one person to tightly squeeze through the edge of the cliffs and then be lowered by rope to the canyon floor 2,000 feet below. The opening would be too small for a wagon to pass through and the thought of chiseling and breaking through the one hundred-foot thick by thirty-foot high slab of rock, seemed impossible. Lyman said, "Some of our party are of the opinion that a road could be made if plenty of money was furnished, but most of us are satisfied that there is no use of this company undertaking to get through the San Juan this way." The comment struck Charles hard, having just completed a six-week wagon trip. Lyman then said, "We've got another group going into the backcountry to the south to see if there is another way for us to get down to the Colorado River and across." And with that report, Charles returned to Jane and shared his new concern about the trip.

Jane remained speechless as she listened to Charles describe the circumstances. She had more questions than he had answers, and both would have to wait patiently for Lyman's report. Together, they took their children to a dinner and dance that had been arranged for the travelers in order to meet each other. Making new acquaintances within the cupped walls of the Dance Hall Rock seemed to alleviate much of the tension surrounding the frustrating news. Although most of the members of the expedition were strangers to each other, several had ties that stretched across the plains and the Atlantic Ocean. Most of these stalwarts, like Charles and Jane, were young married couples with small children. There were a few unmarried men and some older campers who accompanied the group. The oldest member of the group was fifty-nine-year-old Jens Nielsen who led the majority of the settlers to the meeting spot at Dance Hall Rock. Before the travelers embarked on the expedition, the temporal and spiritual leadership of the group was placed on the shoulders of Silas Smith.

While the adults were aware there was a possibility of failure until the scouting parting returned the next day, there was nothing they could do about it until morning. The children were unaware of the seriousness of the situation and the adults decided to let the youngsters enjoy the evening celebration before the inevitable news that would come the next day. There was measured merriment that evening, but the Saints knew it was important to orchestrate a celebration and dance. Charles Walton and Samuel Cox pulled out their fiddles and began playing. Before long, a coronet, trumpet and guitar joined in while everyone, including the children, danced.

After weeks of travel, the opportunity to have some fun was long overdue. The sky was clear, and the moon and stars lit up the nighttime festivities. As the evening wore on, one by one, families prepared to bed down and the sounds of the fiddles gave way to the serenade of nature's night-time music.

The next morning, the travelers awoke to the voices of the returning scouting party. Everyone's fears were confirmed. An alternate route was impossible and turning back was something they didn't want to do. The goal to reach the San Juan Valley now seemed hopeless. Nevertheless, the group decided to go on to the "hole" before making any decisions about quitting and turning back. As the concluding notes rang out from Samuel Cox's morning bugle call, the group gathered together for morning prayers and roll call. With the wagons and livestock readied, the company hesitantly started down the trail toward the "hole." The caravan of wagons, settlers, and livestock stretched over two miles long. It was almost 60 miles from Dance Hall Rock to the "hole" and every step was over rock. From time to time, a small patch of sand and dirt would cushion the horse hooves and make the wagon ride a bit more bearable.

By this time, many wagons were in poor condition and repairs along the trail were a daily occurrence, only aggravated by the rock tundra that refused to give way to horse or wagon, and a washed-out trail that needed to be repaired or avoided. Horses went lame from the terrible conditions. Their hooves cracked and bled from clomping over the uneven rocks. Horse blood stained the rocky ground in numerous places and would serve as a testament of the company's journey for generations to come. Each night, the group tried to uplift each other by holding dances and presenting readings, speeches, and gospel sermons. When the stress was high and the settlers got "short" with each other, dancing seemed to calm everyone down.

As the days dragged on, the settlers pushed and pulled their teams and livestock over steep and slick rock formations that seemed to stretch for miles. Although the temperatures were cool, sweat from exertion poured down the faces of men and women alike. There was little, if any, food for the animals as they made their way across the stone desert. The horses began giving out. Every horizon seemed as if it was the last the animals could conquer. After many days of brutal travel, the first wagons crept over a steep rock summit and shouts of joy echoed across the desert. There, a mile in the distance was the "hole." Word quickly spread from wagon to wagon and a renewed energy surged through the company. The group crossed the last span of rock and sandstone to see before them a rock wall that stretched for miles in both directions. Directly ahead of them the thick wall seemed to have been split by the hand of God, leaving a three-foot wide gap. They had reached the famed Hole in the Rock.

Just as it seemed prayers had been answered and the way had been made clear, the reality of the situation began to sink in. As the trekkers approached the crevice and looked down, they were astounded to see a 2,000-foot chasm leading to the river below. The drop seemed unmerciful and unconquerable. It seemed as if it were a mile to the bottom of the canyon with the steepest drop being at the top of the cliffs where they stood. The first 100 feet appeared to be a complete drop-off. There was a small notch in the canyon wall that was large enough for a man to squeeze through, but certainly not big enough to allow a wagon to pass.

Travel to San Juan by any other route wasn't possible at this point, and to make matters worse, an early winter was threatening. Snow was beginning to fall, and the temperature was dropping dramatically as November came to a close. Although each member of the party had been encouraged to bring a full year supply of necessities, the lack of water, feed for the animals and wood to burn, had placed the settlers in peril. Soon, snowdrifts began to pile up as an unusually heavy winter bore down on the colonizers. Retreat was implausible and suddenly the newly formed company realized they were facing certain calamity. Recognizing these seemingly insurmountable challenges, Silas Smith brought the adults of the group together and told them they needed to make a decision as to which course to take—continue forward or turn back. None in the group felt there was a choice. According to the experienced frontiersmen present, a retreat through the now snow-blocked Escalante Mountains would be impossible. The group realized they were marooned until the next spring melt. Tempers began to flare, and frustration mounted. Smith gathered the leadership of the group near the canyon's rim for a meeting. Many ideas were shared, and opinions were expressed, but every thought boiled down to those same two choices. Smith decided to send a team of explorers a little further on to see if any possible route through the bottom of the canyon could be found, or perhaps built. Charles Walton was one of the members of that group of scouts and within a few hours, the men were scaling down the rock face and onto the canyon floor below. For an entire week the scouts searched the area and then returned to the main camp, exhausted, depressed and ready to give up. Rumors had been spreading throughout the camp that the landscape ahead was extremely gouged by deep gulches and canyons, and no road could possibly be built. The scouting party confirmed the rumors as fact. In speaking to the group, Charles said, "A bird could not fly over the route, let alone taking teams." A cloud of doom fell over the company. Some members began complaining out loud and caused an even greater disruption. Samuel Rowley was overheard stating, "Before we left our homes, we were told that the country had been explored, that the road was feasible. But now we find that someone had been mistaken." Mistaken was an understatement and tension continued to mount.

Silas Smith informed the group that he was going to take immediate advantage of the warm break in the weather and go to Salt Lake City where he could discuss the issue with church officials. He rounded up several horses and placed them in the lead to break through the snow in order to drive his wagon safely through. The additional horses would also be used to expedite his travels. He hastily returned to church headquarters in Salt Lake City where he met with church President John Taylor who had succeeded the recently deceased Brigham Young. President Taylor listened intently to Smith as he relayed the conditions of the settlers at the "hole." Following several minutes of silence, President Taylor told Silas that President Brigham Young personally told him he wanted the San Juan Mission opened. If a prophet of God wanted that area open, he assured, the heavens would ensure the safe travels of the company.

Weeks later, Silas Smith returned to his flock with the news that President Taylor had the utmost confidence in the group and the expedition was deemed imperative by the leading authorities of the Church. He called everyone together to discuss the options. Tensions had flared, but frustrations soon turned to humility as Smith, acting as the presiding church authority, began the meeting. He reminded the group that they were part of a religious movement as well as a pioneer expedition. What transpired next demonstrated the power of shared belief and unified spirit, affirmed by faith. After a word of heartfelt prayer, the adult members of the group huddled together to discuss their options. Every member of the group was given adequate time to share their thoughts on the predicament and offer any ideas or suggestions. The group then discussed each theory with the hope that at the meeting's conclusion, they would know what course of action should be taken. Within moments, a few people immediately jumped to their feet opining that turning back was the only real choice they had. When it was Jens Nielsen's turn to speak, the patriarch slowly stood up and expressed his appreciation to God and the entire company for the privilege of being in their presence and in this particular circumstance. He then said, "I would like to leave my vote to President Smith and the Lord. But this much I will promise you, that if we are to go on, a road will be made, and a crop will be raised the next season." With that, he quietly sat down and listened.

When everyone had taken an opportunity to speak, President Smith retired to his wagon where he petitioned the Lord for help and direction. A hushed silence fell over the camp while he prayed, and soon he emerged and returned to the group saying he felt inspired they should, "Go after Hole in the Rock!" Smith then asked the members of the camp to raise their hands if they would support his decision. All but a few held up their hands, and the decision was finalized. The entire camp had been strengthened with a unified voice at the testimony meeting, and with the enlistment of God's help they were now prepared to go forward and complete the task to which each believed they were called.

As the vote came to a close a courageous soul broke forth in song and the stillness of the snow-bedecked desert was soon enveloped by the strains of the favorite Mormon hymn, "The Spirit of God."

"The Spirit of God like a fire is burning,
   the Latter-day glory begins to come forth.
The visions and blessings of old are returning,
   and angels are coming to visit the Earth.
We'll sing and we'll shout with the armies of heaven,
   hence forth and forever, Amen and Amen."

Years later, Kumen Jones would say, "Here is where a decision was made that has affected the San Juan Mission for all time. The country would have been settled, but it would've been under a different lineup, for that same bunch could not have been gotten together again."

As the adults returned to their wagons to share the news with their families, Jens Nielsen was overheard to say in his thick Swedish accent, "We will go on whether we can or not. If the Saints had plenty of 'stickie-ta-gudy' we cannot fail." There was no longer any discussion of turning back. The spiritually buoyed trekkers would be spending the Christmas of 1879 overlooking Glen Canyon and the meandering river snaking some two thousand feet below their view. As they worked in unified purpose, more lifelong friendships were forged.

Chapter Eleven
"Fire in the Hole"

After heartfelt discussions, prayer, and a final decision, the Saints went to work building a road down the cliff. Each evening as the sun would drop below the rocky furrows to the west, the settlers would be back to work preparing their evening meals and organizing what tools they had for the monumental task that lay ahead of them. Bands of young children could be seen running across the horizon as they scoured the landscape in search of a coal-like black rock called schadscale that was used for fuel. Since wood was a scarcity and the schadscale, which proved to be an inefficient fuel source, was difficult to find, the pioneers found themselves relying on cooking over the "plains proven" dried cow manure. The older children would search for twigs and prairie grass that was used for cooking, or to feed the livestock. The bundles of twigs, when combined with the schadscale, could provide a small blaze for as long as a half an hour.

As the weeks passed, food became scarce. Young Charlie and his sister, Maggie, would lead the family's livestock miles into the never-ending clusters of rock, in search of any blade of grass that the animals could chew. The horse feed that many of the pioneers brought with them was ground into flour and consumed by humans, not the intended livestock. Even dried out corn became a staple food as the pioneers experienced rationing that they thought had been left behind on the plains 25 years earlier. With all these challenges, the evenings remained a favorite time as cares were cast aside and the group enjoyed music and dancing to the fiddles of Charles Walton and Samuel Cox.

As the winter temperatures turned bitter, the company's shelters had to be improvised. To guard against the cold, wagon covers were reinforced using ingenious methods. One family placed a hand-woven rug over the cover to provide extra insulation. They sewed pockets into the cover and used them to store their brushes, combs, medicine, towels, washcloths and other necessary items. Another family removed the wagon wheels so that the bed of the wagon was closer to the ground where it could take advantage of the natural insulation. With each challenge that nature threw at the settlers, a solution equal to the problem could be figured out. Many would later say that it was those challenges that made the members of the expedition sure they could handle any obstacle they came across. Each day, as the children searched for fuel for fires and food for livestock, the women of the camp prepared adequate meals from limited and rationed resources. Periodically, a welcomed treat of sage chicken or deer would be killed to supplement their rations. As winter progressed, some of the livestock became too weak to survive. Those animals were harvested for the good of the camp.

More than fifty men worked daily to enlarge the crevice called "the hole," from a three-foot wide fissure to one more than ten feet across in order to get a wagon through its narrow opening. Widening the "hole" was in reality the least of their problems. Once wagons could pass through the opening, they faced a terribly steep drop-off, falling over fifty feet to a small but fairly level landing below. Several perpendicular ledges below the opening constituted the immediate problem of the company. The diminished provisions and lack of necessities to build the road to the river became an even bigger issue. At first, the workers used blasting powder to widen the gap, but even with dynamite, the work was slow, tedious and perilous.

Most of the rock wall sealed the route, and some of the cliff had to be blasted away from the ridgeline in order to make passage off the top edge possible. The rock was more than one hundred feet thick and taller than 4 wagons stacked on top of each other. After each blast, the men spent days breaking the rock apart and throwing it off the cliffs or hauling it out of the "hole." There were only a few men in the entire region that understood the capabilities and dangers of blasting power. The process of blasting rock away without injuring workers or weakening rock that needed to remain intact was as much an art as it was a science. Within a few weeks of his return to the "hole," Silas Smith had engaged the services of Ben and Hyrum Perkins from one of the communities near Escalante. The senior Perkins boy was affectionately known as, "the blower and blaster from Wales." These men had extensive blasting experience from their days working in the mines in the United Kingdom and Smith had been fortunate to run into the brothers on his return trip from Salt Lake.

After surveying the site, the Perkins brothers got to work blasting the rock away. Wisdom and sure-footedness were required when working near the blasting area since the ground was extremely treacherous. The trail across the top of the cliffs to the worksite was covered with loose rock and small patches of grass. During the winter, it was slippery and wet. On more than one occasion horses slipped off the edge, falling eighteen hundred feet or more to be dashed upon the rocks below. As the work progressed and the blasting became more precise, it became necessary for the Perkins brothers to hang from a rope and pack the blasting powder into the cracks along the face of the cliff. Several men had to secure the lines to keep the men from falling to their deaths. As the rope was lengthened to dangle the men further down the cliff's sides, it also became weaker. This made it necessary to find a lighter weight person to pack the blasting powder into the rocks. The Perkins brothers looked throughout the camp for a person they thought could handle the task and chose, none other than, the young Charlie Walton.

Upon hearing the news, Jane's immediate reaction was, "Absolutely not!" She shuddered at the very thought of having her young son lowered over the 2,000-foot cliffs with a satchel full of volatile blasting powder. Charlie thought the prospect of working with the blasting powder was exciting and working with the men was certainly a marker that he was also becoming a man. Jane would never be convinced that Charlie's involvement in the blasting effort was a good idea, but with her husband's coaxing, she finally relented. She refused to venture near the cliff's edge whenever Charlie was working with the blasting powder and dynamite, and certainly not when he was tethered to a long rope hanging halfway down the cliff.

Each day, Charlie Walton would finish his chores with the livestock, eat his lunch, and then join the men on the face of the cliff. Once there, he would spend his afternoons hanging from a long and weathered rope, placing explosive powder in rock crevices. By the end of the day, he would have terrible red sores caused by the rough ropes scratching and rubbing against his body. After packing two or three crevices with blasting powder, Charlie would shout up to the men holding the rope to pull him up the face of the cliff. Once he was safely above the cliff, the words, "fire in the hole" would serve as the only warning before blasting. From there, the fuse would be lit and every person near the scene would pause from their labors long enough to watch the burning fuse tumble and twist across the rock as its thick column of smoke swirled around the bright and bubbling flame. As the fuse neared the blasting powder, folks would cover their ears until the explosion ended. At times, the blasting powder would be so well placed that rock would be thrown far enough from the walls of the canyon that it would create a huge splash in the river below. Once the rock had been blown from the canyon walls it would leave larger and much more manageable pockets that needed excavating. Much of the rock would be carried below and used for road grade on the steep incline. If the supply of blasting powder ran low, the settlers would have to rely on the freezing nighttime temperatures to help them break the face of the cliffs apart. On those particularly cold days, Charlie would be looped over the edge to fill the cracks and holes in the canyon walls with water. When the water froze it would expand and cause the rock to break loose. Often, the cracks would be large enough to insert sticks of dynamite, which would then be exploded.

Unfortunately, the blasting powder and the dynamite supply was used up long before the road down to the river was completed. The tired cadre of workers had to resort to more manual forms of labor in order to complete the job. The men continued the daily routine of expanding the gorge and as the work progressed, the pioneers began to see the "light at the end of the tunnel." A decision was made to send another scouting party out to map the road that would be taken once the company descended the cliffs, and four men began their journey on the 7th of December 1879. The four scouters carried their supplies on two packing burro's and two riding horses. They anticipated the trip would take 8 days to travel the roughly 70 miles. George Hobbs was one of the men chosen for this expedition because he was familiar with the countryside, but unfortunately, within the first couple of days, the party lost their way. Having no trail to follow, the men worked their way along the riverbank and the steep canyon walls. They eventually reached Castle Gulch where they picked up a known trail that led to Clay Hill Pass, about 40 miles from the hole. They traveled for another two days before becoming snowed in near Elk Mountain. Eight inches of snow fell on them and hid the trail. They were lost, out of food and desperately cold. The men knew it was Christmas day, and their families would be expecting their return. Unfortunately, they knew they wouldn't be returning that day. Each day and night, the settlers petitioned God to help them through the difficulties they were facing and for the safe return of the overdue scouting party.

The band of settlers celebrated Christmas day, 1879, in two different locations. The settlers at the top of the "hole" awoke to six inches of new snow that had blanketed the Escalante Valley overnight, and the children wasted no time in scurrying from their wagons to play in the cold, white powder. By afternoon, the snow had melted, and water lay pooled in natural basins scattered across the sandstone ground. The settlers busied themselves by scooping up the water and storing it in barrels and buckets for drinking. There were no Christmas gifts nor special meals that Christmas day, but later in the evening there would be some music and dancing. For the families of the four scouts who were lost, the evening was not spent in revelry but in heartfelt prayer.

The following day, the scouting party made their way past landmarks called Salvation Knoll and Comb Wash. They were out of food and after their third day of forced fasting, they carved their names in a rock with the date and their circumstances, not knowing if they'd survive much longer. On December 28th, 1879 the scouting party wandered into a peaceful valley where the lights from a cabin welcomingly reached out to them. They had finally found what would soon become Bluff. The occupants of the cabin were the Harris family from Colorado. They fed the men and gave them a comfortable place to sleep for the night.

The next morning, the men awoke, thanked the Harris family, and then set about returning to the "hole". The return trip took 11 days and was just as difficult as the outbound leg. They continued to experience blinding snowstorms, unrelenting fog, slush, and rain. Even with their light provisions, hunger was a constant enemy, and the rugged countryside challenged their every footstep. Not only did the men suffer, but so did their horses. The horses' hooves were worn completely to the padding and each step on the rocks left circles of blood. On New Year's Day 1880, 23 days after leaving the "hole," they walked back into their camp amid rounds of applause and tears. The mission was complete—the scouts knew the path they would use to lead the settlers along after they conquered the Hole in the Rock.

As the blasting and breaking away of the "hole" at the top of the canyon neared completion, the creation of a road down the canyon walls and below the cliffs began. Grooves wide enough for wagon wheels were cut into the sides of the rock walls in order for the upper cliff-side wagon wheels to keep the wagons from tipping over during their downward trip. Stakes were then pounded into the canyon walls and jutted out two feet in order to widen the dugway. These were called "shelf roads." Foliage and wood were then laid over the stakes to build a bridge-like structure against the canyon wall. Finally, a wooden track was built at the bottom of the "hole" around a large gulch. The gulch had to be filled with boulders and other debris to make it level enough for the wagons to continue the last part of the journey to the river's edge.

On January 26, 1880, after two months of grueling work, the perilous route was ready for passage. As the first wagon and team was brought to the edge of the "hole," the horses started to buck and push back. The animals refused to go down the first part of the trail, which was affectionately called, "the chute." The chute dropped about fifty feet, nearly straight down. When team after team refused to start down the chute, even with the pushing and prodding of the men, doubts surfaced as to whether or not the wagons could be taken. It was then that camp member Joe Barton approached the front of the wagon line and offered to send his team down first. A hushed discussion ensued as President Silas Smith considered the offer. Finally agreeing, two men hooked Barton's horses up to the first wagon belonging to Hyrum Perkins. Barton climbed onto the wagon's seat and snapped his reins. The dutiful horses complied. With the rear wagon wheels locked to keep them from turning, 10 men, (five on each side of the back of the wagon) pulled on ropes to help hold the wagon back from tumbling down the drop off. Gingerly, the team placed one foot in front of the other off the 40-degree decline, and slowly but surely, made their way down the slippery rock face. At times, the team would get spooked, but Barton would calm the horses by talking to them in quiet, gentle tones. The horses would then continue down the difficult grade, each step carefully measured. It seemed it was no coincidence that a year earlier, Barton's horses had become completely blind due to being afflicted with pink eye. Barton had patiently cared for the team and they had learned to have complete trust in their master. The horses listened and responded to his voice without trepidation.

One by one, the other horses followed the lead. Wagons, people and livestock inched their way down the perilous canyon walls to the bottom. Kumen Jones recalled. "I had a well-broken team and hitched it on to B. Perkins wagon and drove it down through the hole. Long ropes were provided and about twenty men and boys held on to the wagons to make sure that there would be no accidents, through [brakes] giving way, or horses cutting up after their long lay-off, but all went smooth and safe." The wagons were lowered using a system of ropes, combined with horsepower and blistered manpower. It was a frightening sight.

Elizabeth M. Decker wrote, "Coming down the hole in the rock to get to the river … is almost strait (sic) down, the cliffs on each side are five hundred feet high and there is just room enough for a wagon to go down. It nearly scared me to death. The first wagon I saw go down they put the brake on and … [chained the rear wheels together so they slid as a unit instead of rolled] and had a big rope fastened to the wagon and about ten men holding back on it and they went down like they would smash everything. I'll never forget that day."

The 26th and final wagon to descend from the Hole in the Rock was that belonging to the Joseph Stanford Smith family. Throughout the day, Smith had joined the other men in tying rope and holding back the other wagons as they tipped off the cliff and started their journey down the 2,000-foot wall. After each wagon arrived safely at the bottom of the canyon, the contingency of men would climb back up the mountain and repeat the process. This time Smith climbed alone, not realizing the other men were not following. As he made his way to the top of the cliffs to take his turn in piloting his wagon down the mountain, he noticed that he and his family were alone at the top. Thinking they were stranded, Stanford and his wife Belle decided to bring the wagon down themselves. With the decision made, Belle sat her three-year-old son on a quilt she had laid on the ground and placed their infant child between his legs. She told the boy not to move until their father returned to get them. She instructed their oldest child, Ada, to stand in front of her brothers as the family said a prayer. Stanford then climbed onto the bench of the wagon as Belle tied one of the horses to the back of the wagon thinking it could pull backwards to slow the momentum until they reached the first ledge. Belle's job would be to steady the anchor horse and continue to urge it to pull against the weight of the wagon as it moved down the cliff. Smith braced his legs against the footboard of the wagon and gently urged the horses forward. As soon as the lead horse stepped off the edge, the wagon lurched and pulled the anchor horse to the ground. Belle struggled to stay on her feet but stumbled, eventually falling on the jagged rocks. Both Belle and the anchor horse were dragged along the steep slope. When the wagon finally stopped, Belle discovered her leg had been torn from heel to hip by jagged rocks. Smith had been intent on steering the horse team and wagon to the bottom of the cliff, he was completely unaware of the situation behind the wagon. Once they reached the valley floor, Smith turned around to see if his wife was all right. He was mortified to see his wife's condition. With pioneer fortitude, Belle told him she had 'crow-hopped' all the way down. Smith helped Belle into the wagon and cleaned and dressed the cut on her leg. Belle was more concerned about their horse at the rear of the wagon. Smith checked it out and saw that the horse was dazed but still alive. He took his hat off and waved it in the air as a salute to his courageous wife. Smith once again climbed to the top of the "hole" to retrieve his children. He carried his infant son down the canyon with his other son and daughter holding on to his sturdy grip. Smith and his wife had miraculously guided their wagon down the opening alone. Once every wagon was delivered to the bottom of the cliff, Charles and Jane spent a few solitary moments looking up through the gash that was Hole-in-the Rock. From this angle it became apparent to them that this small band of pioneers had just experienced an extraordinary miracle.

That night, Charles Sr. finally sat down to write in his journal. "So we went on from the Hole in the Rock and commenced to build a road across the Colorado River," he matter-of-factly penned.

What was thought in the beginning to be the quickest route to the San Juan Valley ended up being much longer than anyone expected. The journey should have been an overland trip by wagon but ended up being an engineering feat that would require months of work using dynamite, picks, axes, chisels and shovels to ensure success. The route through the Hole in the Rock was expected to cut hundreds of miles off of the trip to San Juan when, in reality, it nearly doubled the distance the pioneers had to travel. The journey that was to last 6 weeks was off by more than five months. The only benefit the journey through the "hole" provided was the avoidance of hostile Indians. Miraculously, no lives were lost and, three children were born along the way. Part of Jens Nielson's prophesy had come true. The settlers had built a road through Hole in the Rock and were on their way to their new home in the San Juan Valley. However, whether his prophesy of producing a successful crop in the new homestead was yet to be seen.

For several more weeks the travelers made their way up and over and down and back through the towering Colorado River canyons and the Comb Mountains. Along the way, the group camped at a place called Salvation Knoll where they were approached by a Ute Indian who wanted to know where they had traveled from. Charles explained they had come through the Colorado River Canyon from

Escalante. He then described how they lowered each of their wagons and 1,000 head of livestock off the ridge. The Indian accused him of being a liar. He indignantly said such a crossing was impossible and left. The settlers knew otherwise.

Chapter Twelve
Bluff

    The exhilaration that accompanied the incredible feat of passing through Hole in the Rock was quickly dashed as the group realized they had many more difficult days of travel ahead of them. They were exhausted, discouraged and hungry. The wagons were falling apart, and the animals could go no further. The group had traveled miles to Hole in the Rock and they knew they had many miles to go before they reached the San Juan Valley. Although the entire trip was about 125 miles long, the travelers had covered more than 260 miles as they zig-zagged over rocks and crevices.

    Facing a barren land of sagebrush with very little water or grass for livestock, and with provisions running low, the group continued to push forward. As the company inched closer and closer to the San Juan, spirits began to lift. The weather-beaten pioneers began to feel immense gratitude that they had been blessed with relatively good health and had escaped serious injury or death along their journey

On April 6th, 1880 the group finally trudged into the small, isolated valley that would become their new home. In wonderment, they slowly scanned the astonishing red sandstone cliffs and towering rock formations that surrounded it. Many became disappointed when they realized the area was much smaller than they had expected. The small strip of land was about a mile wide and was surrounded by red cliffs rising three to four hundred feet high. A small, muddy river ran through its center. The orange backdrop contrasted the dense, green sagebrush of the valley with unique beauty.

As the initial disappointment wore off, the settlers looked for any positive aspects about their new home. They found that while only small parcels of land lay on either side of the river, the soil was actually rich and covered with cottonwood trees. The men knew that cottonwood was not a preferred wood for cabin building but would have to do until more suitable wood could be found. As the negative first impression wore off, ideas for a town name began to circulate. Someone mentioned the beautiful bluffs that surrounded the vale, and the name "Bluff" was chosen.

Although the settlers were completely exhausted from the journey, they knew their work had just begun. The leaders of the company immediately selected a site for the city center and then divided the men and their families into groups and gave out assignments. A few men were put in charge of measuring out 16 acres of farmland for each family. They did this by using lengths of rope. Three other men were given the responsibility of planning an irrigation system to supply water to each parcel of property. Luckily, it was spring, and the climate was mild. Several men began the backbreaking work of digging ditches and moving stone in order for irrigation water to flow into the small valley. The ground the settlers would begin farming sat at an elevation approximately six feet above the river's flow, yet water marks at the river's edge indicated the water, at times, would rise much closer to ground level. Although the land on both sides of the river seemed adequate for farming, a decision was made to use only the northern side of the river for the time being. While farmland was being developed, another group had been given the assignment to plan and build a town center with a surrounding fort. Ferdinand Decker served as surveyor. He accurately recorded that Bluff was located 328 miles south and 126 miles east of Salt Lake City, and then carved the blueprint for the town into the trunk of an old cottonwood tree near the city center. As the land parcels in the town were given out, a few men and women could be heard grumbling that certain families were receiving preferential treatment in the assignment of lots. To avoid any bad blood, the leaders of the company decided to carefully measure each lot at 12 rods, and then have a randomized drawing to determine which family got which lot.

By the close of that first year, the settlers had successfully moved water into the town and built small cabins out of quartered cottonwood logs and aspen trees found several miles away. The summer heat could be stifling so roofs were covered with dirt to help with insulation. The settlers had been advised by the government not to branch out into surrounding areas but to live close together and build a fort for protection from the Indians. Because of this, the cabins were built around the perimeter of the fort with the walls of the fort connecting them. The cabin doors faced the interior. A well was dug inside the fort and clear water was carried in from Cow Canyon for culinary use. Outside of the occasional rainstorms that drifted through the valley, the Blue Mountains that lay forty miles north of Bluff, offered the only source for culinary water for the community. The streams originated high on the snow-covered peaks and flowed most of the year. This would cause dangerous and damaging runoff in the spring. By fall, the water continued to emerge from the small creeks and springs that ran much lower in the valley. The new settlers of Bluff had no idea how much water the Blue Mountains held but were always thankful for its quenching reward.

The new residents did experience many irritations that first year. The irrigation ditches had been dug in unstable ground and unexpected floods made it nearly impossible to keep the water in the ditch for any length of time. The soil turned out to be quite unsuitable for planting and required tedious care and improvement. Irrigation dams broke frequently, transforming the much needed and highly coveted water from a former friend into a tumultuous enemy bent on destroying weeks of work. The extreme heat was not only damaging to the tender crops but to the weary backs of those who toiled under its oppression. The logs used for building the cabins were difficult to fit together and the caulking fixed between them was inefficient. Jane and the other women would spend many hours washing clothes and bedding and cleaning the interior of the cabins after rain leaked through the roofs and streamed through the cracks in the walls. Folks in every household would scramble for barrels and pots to try to catch the water, but the cabins inevitably became a muddy mess. If the rainstorms weren't bad enough, Sandstorms also plagued the community. Each time the wind blew, sand made its way through the cracks and crevices of the cabins and into the food and bedding. Unfortunately, sandstorms were a common occurrence in Bluff. In spite of all the disruptions, Jens Nielson's prophecy soon began to be realized. The settlers heroically grew beautiful crops in the San Juan at the close of that first year. Corn, sugar cane, wheat, oats and barley were all harvested.

Among the first orders of business for the new town was the organization of the First Ward of the Latter-day Saint church. Jens Nielson was called as bishop of the ward and he chose George Sevy and Kumen Jones as his counselors. Silas Smith was authorized by church headquarters in Salt Lake City to organize a Sunday School. Buildings had not yet been constructed, so church meetings were held outdoors, including that first Sunday when townspeople cleared an area near an old swing alongside the San Juan River. From this vantage point, the settlers could see Indians who watched them closely, some on the south side of the river, more on the north. Many of the members of the community felt uneasy as they conducted their religious services in open view of the Indians. Some expressed concern that being so visible advertised which settlers were attending services and which had remained at home. It only took a few months for the citizens to construct a multipurpose meetinghouse where the saints could hold weekly church services, civic meetings and political functions. During the weekdays, the meetinghouse also served as a school and Charles Walton was appointed to be the town's first teacher.

Soon, with the stamp of approval from the territorial governor, the town of Bluff and the county of San Juan was established. With such a small population, many of the men and women were given multiple responsibilities in the civic operations of the town. Charles was no exception. Along with his farming and teaching duties, Charles was appointed as the first county clerk and county treasurer. He also operated the first post office and was named postmaster. It was also necessary for the members of the community to have multiple responsibilities within the Church. With the formation of the area's first "stake," (a large organizational unit attesting to growth among the Latter-day Saints), Charles willingly accepted the call to be the stake clerk. With all these important responsibilities, he somehow found the time to play his fiddle for the community dances. Jane was called to serve as the president of the ward's Relief Society, the Church's organization for women. This responsibility put her in a buggy or on horseback frequently as she checked on the welfare of the women in Bluff and the surrounding county. At times, Jane's duties would take her as far away as Moab, more than one hundred miles away. Regardless of the assignment she bore, Jane fulfilled it with tenacity and perfectionism. To Jane, completing a job ahead of schedule or more efficiently than she had previously done was a personal quest that often led to working many more hours than were required.

Along with his many duties, Charles enjoyed organizing and directing dramatic programs. He also enjoyed performing in them. The small meetinghouse in the fort was a perfect place to entertain. It consisted of one room furnished with wooden benches that sat 40 to 50 people. At the front of the room was a small, slightly elevated stage. There was a door at the back of the stage leading outside that was perfect for performers to enter and exit. Charles would direct plays, build scenery, gather costumes and even clean the meetinghouse after the programs. The performances were a welcome respite from the daily grind of hard work.

On the weekdays, school children would file into the building to begin their lessons using books, mostly delivered at the hands of benefactors from the community. They became a treasured part of the school's supplies. Charles usually taught lessons with the children memorizing recitations. On Sundays the meetinghouse turned into a house of worship where the Saints gathered to take the sacrament, sing hymns, listen to sermons and receive instruction.

Although the farms in Bluff were beginning to thrive, Charles found that it was not enough to keep the family fed. One day he decided to join many other men to seek work outside Bluff. The settlers were struggling, and many of the men left for lengthy periods of time looking for any kind of work to supplement their family's income. By the end of the first year, 21 wagons had left for southwestern Colorado carrying men in search of work on roads, railroads, sawmills, ranches, freighting or anything they could find. Charles hated leaving Jane and their children alone in Bluff. Many men had already left, and it seemed like a ghost town with only a few older men and the women left to care for the community. Eventually, Charles and Jane decided to go without many "wants" in order to minimize the time Charles would have to be away.

The hardship created by unemployment also caused many of Bluff's families to leave in search of a more suitable location to live. Jane and Charles both considered leaving as well. Word about the struggles the Saints were experiencing in Bluff reached Salt Lake City. Elder Joseph F. Smith, from church headquarters in Salt Lake City, visited the town to look into the problems. He came to assess the situation and release the settlers from their responsibility to settle the San Juan Valley—if he deemed it necessary. After evaluating the problems and listening to the townspeople's complaints, Elder Smith brought the settlers together and released all who wished to leave. He said, "Those that wish to move away are released with the blessings of the presidency of the Church, but those that stay and hold the mission should be eternally blessed." After these words, only a few members moved away while the rest stayed. Elder Smith then personally asked Charles and Jane if they would stay, considering he was county clerk and stake clerk. Once again Jane and Charles responded affirmatively to the Church's request and they continued to make Bluff their home.

After Elder Smith's visit, the Walton family's life in Bluff returned to its regular routine. Each weekday Charles taught school and each Sunday the family attended church. Again, the monotony of daily life was broken up with various kinds of entertainment as Charles continued to organize and direct skits and musicals. He and Samuel Cox would play their fiddles for dances that were attended by both young and old. Jane loved to dance and rarely missed one. She especially loved watching Charles perform. Many times, during a town celebration, local cowboys would come to look on and occasionally participate. Sometimes troublemakers had to be restrained. Town picnics were another form of fun as families prepared their own lunches and rode to the picnic grounds next to the river. The townsfolk would climb the red rocks toward a naturally eroded formation in Cow Canyon called, "the ballroom." Here, they would hold dances surrounded by the canyon's sandstone walls and spiraling high cliffs where the natural acoustics made the music resonate and echo. Young people enjoyed gathering around the old swing tree by the river on balmy evenings.

The Saints enthusiastically celebrated Independence Day in July. As the day approached, Charles would orchestrate programs and celebrations that would last the entire day. At 9:00 am each July 4th, the townspeople would fill the meetinghouse and Charles would have someone read the Declaration of Independence. He also organized and directed a town choir, followed by a few orations and some music. He usually included a comic reading in the program to keep the spirit of the day lighthearted. After lunch, the children would enjoy a dance organized just for them while the adults prepared for their own dance later that evening, after the children were put to bed. These celebrations would be repeated a few weeks later on July 24th as the town celebrated the anniversary of the first company of pioneer's arrival in the Salt Lake Valley.

Although Bluff was farther from the railroad than any settlement in the entire west, as each year passed, it became more established and distinct. The townspeople began building large homes with sandstone blocks cut out of the cliffs. The town boasted its own molasses mill that processed the sugar cane grown in the area, and the settlers proudly built a stone church to replace the old log meetinghouse. One frightful night after the church had been dedicated, a fierce rainstorm came barreling through the canyon. Intense lightning and thunder echoed off the red cliffs. Without warning, lightning struck the church. Although the church was left standing after the ordeal, it had been damaged structurally and had to be torn down a few years later.

While challenges were faced each day, the community of Bluff continued to grow, and the citizens grew more committed to the town's success. The settlers were frequently dealing with issues involving the Indians in the area and looked to church leadership for advice. Brigham Young had instructed: "Feed the Indians, instead of fighting them," and they had followed his policy as best they could. This instruction worked to a degree, but there were still provocations by renegades that were almost beyond endurance. Bluff had become a hotbed of Indian predation, especially from the Paiutes, and a sidetrail for desperados avoiding the law. Many times, the Indians stole the settlers' cattle and fights erupted over hunting or land.

One Sunday, Jane was not feeling well and decided to stay home from church. Charles felt uneasy about leaving her alone, but Jane insisted that he take the children and go without her. She told him she was just going to rest in bed, and she would be fine. Not long after the family left, Jane laid down on her bed to try to get some sleep. Suddenly, she heard a quiet knock at the door. This seemed very odd to her since she knew everyone would be in church. Although she was feeling ill, she opened the door and was startled to see an Indian standing in front of her. The Indian stepped inside and told her he was hungry and wanted food. Jane's heart began to race but she did not dare make any threatening moves. Instead, she prepared a simple meal for the man and waited as he ate. Once fed, the Indian seemed satisfied and was about to leave when he noticed Jane's wedding band on her finger. He told her he wanted it and ordered her to take it off. Since the day of her marriage, the ring had never been off Jane's finger and the fit had become too tight to be removed. The Indian grabbed her hand and they both fell to the floor in a struggle.

As Charles sat in church with his children listening to the sermons, he became uneasy. He whispered to the children that he must go home and check on their mother. He quietly snuck out the door at the back of the church and rushed home. As he approached their cabin, he noticed the door was ajar and he could hear some sort of commotion from within. When he entered the house, he found Jane on the floor fighting with the Indian. Charles grabbed the man, threw him out the door and watched as the assailant fled into the trees. The Indian was never seen again, and Charles figured he had just been traveling through.

Despite all its challenges, Jane and Charles loved living next to the San Juan River in Bluff. They raised their children, Charles Jr., Magnolia and Leona, within view of the distinctive Locomotive Rock, known for its resemblance to an oncoming train, and the Twin Rocks, symbols of twins from a Navajo legend.

In 1884, just as it seemed many of the challenges in Bluff had been overcome, disaster struck. After a winter of unusually heavy snowfall, the spring runoff flowed nine feet higher than normal. The sandstone-laden floodwaters destroyed many of the cabins and ruined farmland. Jane and Charles watched as the torrent destroyed the land they had worked so hard to farm. The Waltons would be forced to spend the next several years re-cultivating the farmland until it began to once again yield favorable crops.

In March 1887, Charles took his son, Charlie, and joined a party of men headed for an area called North Montezuma to help scout out a more hospitable land to settle. The area was 40 miles north of Bluff and could be reached in about two days. North Montezuma was located at the foot of a small mountain range called the Blue Mountains, named for its misty blue appearance created by shadows. The valley was much bigger than Bluff and was covered with vegetation that was fed by crystal clear mountain streams. Charles Sr. and a man named George Adams immediately began the search for the water's source. The two followed the streams up the mountain a few miles until they came upon their origin. They were thrilled to complete this important task and posted stakes declaring their right to all of the water that ran east of the mountains. The next day however, they were disappointed to learn that the Carlisle Cattle Company had already made a claim for the water. Settlers were familiar with Carlisle's cowboys and had experienced conflict over rangeland and water in the past. The company's cow hands were tough and seasoned. Many were wanted criminals from across the west, a fearsome and dangerous bunch. They served as the company's first line of defense in protecting the herd from marauding Indians.

In a show of good faith, Mr. Carlisle surprisingly relinquished his claim of the water rights on the Blue Mountain to the Saints. With the water issue resolved, Charles helped the men plant crops and mark out a new settlement they called the Montezuma Mission. Earlier that year, Charles and a few men from Bluff had traveled to New Mexico to purchase seeds with funds they had received from the Church. When the men returned to North Montezuma, they planted the seeds and then set out to build some cabins. One of the cabins would be used later in the season to store the bounty from the crops that were in the ground. The men were elated to find a large abundance of trees on the Blue Mountain, very suitable for building the cabins and completing other construction projects.

During July of 1887, peace between the Carlisle Company and the settlers soured. Tensions mounted as the cowboys and the settlers found themselves in continuous conflict over land and water. The cowboys didn't like having the "squatters" in their rangeland and the settlers, in-turn, didn't like the bullying by the cowboys. The settlers began to be fearful of the rising contention and sent an envoy to Fort Lewis in Colorado to enlist the help of the United States government. The Latter-day Saints were not accustomed to seeking or receiving help from the government but felt they had no other choice. The U.S. Army deployed a garrison to the Soldier Springs area near the base of the Blue Mountains to enforce laws and quell problems. But once the garrison left, pockets of conflict and threats sprang up again between the cowboys and the Navajo, Ute and Paiute Indians. Because of the tension, the group of Saints stayed just outside the North Montezuma area in a place called Verdure.

Although the men were away from their homes and families, they continued to hold church meetings every Sunday—each taking turns teaching and preaching. From time to time, the men's families would make the trek northward to visit for a week or two. On other occasions, when the workload permitted, the men made the journey home to be with their families and help in the many chores left undone while they had been gone. For the spouses and children left behind in Bluff, there was a tremendous burden placed on them to care for their property, livestock and crops without the man of the house there to help.

The additional burdens of managing farms in two different locations became too taxing for many families and some suggested it was time to leave Bluff and head north to build new homesteads. For Jane and Charles Walton, this wasn't an option. They had committed to their church leaders that they would stay until their release came and that was what they intended on doing. Jane and Charles decided to stay in Bluff a few more years in order to keep the community they had helped to establish intact. While Jane took care of the affairs in Bluff, Charles worked tirelessly in Montezuma preparing for the harvest and his eventual return home to Jane and the family in Bluff.

When it came time to harvest the crops in Montezuma, Charles and the other men had to complete the work by hand. They weren't able to rely on the modern threshers Charles' family had built. Of the five that had been constructed, none were in the area and Charles hadn't had the time or resources to build one since arriving in the San Juan Valley. The men set about cutting the grain with a scythe— a sword like blade attached to a long wooden handle. When swung left to right, the blade would cut through the grain stalk and the plant would tumble to the ground. It was a difficult and tedious task but until more convenient harvesting methods could be obtained, it would have to do. The men would then tie up the grain stalks by hand, creating a bundle, which was called a "shook" or "sheave". Since rope was a scarce commodity, the sheaves of grain were often tied together using other strands of the plant. These small bundles were then stood upright to dry the grain. Once the stalks were dried, they were spread onto the ground and beat with an instrument called a flail. The flail was made of two pieces of wood that were tied together with leather. One piece of wood was used as the handle and the other piece was used for striking the grain to break it from the stalk. The remaining mixture of grain and chaff was then tossed into the air when there was a breeze. The breeze would carry away the chaff and leave the golden nuggets of grain behind, a process called winnowing. After a few weeks, the harvest was complete.

At the conclusion of that first summer, the men of the Montezuma Mission had successfully built a log house, a cellar, several corrals and stockyards. The crops they had planted grew well, and by the end of that first year they were able to store 2,500 bushels of wheat, 100 bushels of oats, barley, vegetables and hay. Buildings and shelters were constructed to store the bounty and after careful consideration, a seemingly friendly cowboy was hired to guard the settlement through the fall and winter.

The men triumphantly returned to Bluff, tired, but optimistic about the head start they would have the following spring when they returned.

Chapter Thirteen
Posey

As the influx of white men living around William Posey increased, so did many legends and horror stories about the Indian. Posey had continued his barrage of killings throughout the southeastern Utah territory during the 1880s. There were many attempts by the United States Army, the Territorial Marshal, and the San Juan County Marshall to capture or kill him—but all failed. Posey began referring to himself as Chief Posey, although it is unknown if the Paiute Nation ever recognized him as a chief.

While the Saints had been establishing the settlement in Bluff, Posey and his good friend Poke would watch cautiously from the hilltops as the settlers leveled an area near the San Juan River and held church meetings. Posey found it odd, almost humorous, that the settlers would leave their livestock and their homes unprotected each Sunday while they met together. As the weeks passed, the renegade

Indian took advantage of the settlers' naivety and began preying on their livestock while they were away at worship. He had managed to steal a horse and kill a few cows for his tribe to eat and was never pursued for the crimes. William Posey was intrigued and captivated by the settlers and their seemingly bounteous possessions.

Problems between "Gentile", or non "Mormon", settlers and the Ute and Paiute Indians had intensified and in 1880, the Doloros Colorado Newspaper published an article titled, "New Indian War." It reported, "Newspaper comments on his actions has but little weight with the average Ute. It neither breaks his heart nor shuts off his wind . . . . Explosive bullets have more influence with savages than folios of vigorous editorials. We cannot appeal to an Indian's sense of justice or cause him to feel the pangs of remorse. Let us substitute Winchester rifles for brains and note the results." A terrible chasm had been created between the Indians and the non-Latter-day Saint white settlers who began to migrate into the area. The Latter-day Saint settlers refused to be a part of the rift—remembering Brigham Young's counsel to feed, rather than fight the Indians. The Paiute Indians, in particular, recognized the efforts of the Saints. While one or more white people were killed each year in Indian attacks, the Latter-day Saints had not been listed in that number. A year after the article was printed, a conflict called "The Pinhook Battle" took place involving a group of Indians, including Mancos Jim, Poke and Posey, who had stolen several horses from a rancher. A posse was called out to search for the horse thieves but was ambushed by a large number of Indians who had come to the defense of the three marauders. A bloody battle ensued, and a large number of both white men and Indians were wounded or killed. Poke bragged that he had personally killed three white men. Years later, in a June 16, 1886 article in the "Idea," a Durango Newspaper, Mancos Jim boasted about the battle. He said, "Dave Willis never took shelter but stood out in bold relief and fought till he fell dead. The other boys tried to protect themselves by getting into a shallow arroyo or washout, they were surrounded and when the Indians charged from one site, hanging onto the ponies, yelling and shooting, the white boys would [rise up] to fire. The Indians in ambush in another direction [would] shoot them down. The white boys were extravagant with their ammunition, which they exhausted about dusk after fighting all day, and the Indians then rode around the washout in a circle, shooting into the living and lifeless bodies till there was not a sign of life in the bloody pit." Like Mancos Jim, Posey flaunted his involvement in the deaths and spoke fondly of the battle because it was there that he met his future wife, Toorah.

Toorah was the sister of Posey's best friend, Poke. During the Pinhook Battle, Posey saw Toorah running from intense gunfire. He grabbed the squaw and helped her find cover until the battle was over, and it wasn't long before a relationship bloomed. Poke did not approve of Posey's relationship with his sister and he had his family kidnap and hide her in order to keep the two apart. For weeks, Posey searched for Toorah and eventually found her being held captive by her brothers in a teepee deep in the forest. Posey laid in wait one night until the brothers were asleep and crept cautiously into the teepee. Posey untied the woman and together they escaped quietly into the night. A few days later, Poke learned of his friend's actions, and decided to accept the love affair. He told Posey he would give his sister in marriage in exchange for 10 horses and some cooking supplies. Posey accepted the deal, knowing he could steal hundreds of horses from the white man. Within a few weeks, Posey and Toorah were married.

Posey and Toorah enjoyed relatively peaceful years together and the only crimes Posey committed were stealing horses and killing the settlers' cattle. The marriage seemed to have a taming effect on him, and most of his time was spent with Toorah. The two truly seemed to be in love with each other and by the mid 1880s they had had two sons, Jesse and Anson. Both Posey and Toorah had a good sense of humor and liked to tease each other. One day, as the two relaxed in their teepee, Posey ordered Toorah to get out of the teepee and round up their horses. This was a common joke between the two with part of the joke being that Toorah would tell Posey, "No!" Toorah's defiance would start an argument between them until both would end up laughing. This day however, when Toorah said, "No," Posey picked up what he thought was an empty revolver and teasingly said, "Get the horse, or I shoot." Once again, she said, "No." In a joking manner, Posey pointed the revolver at Toorah and pulled the trigger. To his horror, the weapon discharged, firing a bullet that struck Toorah in the stomach. Terrified, Posey ran to Bluff and asked the settlers for help. A woman named Jody Wood accompanied him back to his teepee and cared for Toorah throughout the day and night. All the time, Posey remained at her side apologizing. By morning, Toorah had died. With a hopeless heart, Posey carried her body to a ledge above a canyon where he had piled a large quantity of wood. He carefully laid Toorah's body on top of the woodpile and set fire to it. He stoically watched as the flames and intense heat consumed her. The fire burned throughout the day. Later that evening he killed Toorah's favorite horse, knowing she would need it in order to ride into the afterlife.

Toorah's death had a profound influence on Posey's personality and his disposition became even harsher than before. As punishment for his sisters' death, Chief Poke ordered Posey to marry Toorah's plain and less desirable sister, and Posey agreed. Together, they had many children, but Posey never felt the happiness he had experienced with Toorah. Even with another marriage and companion, Posey's disposition only worsened. As the years passed, he was involved in many more incidents of bloodshed and gun battles.

The settlers did all they could to keep harmony with their native neighbors. For them, the occasional loss of a cow or horse was a meager price to pay for continued peace and safety. Knowing that the Indians were strategic in much of their plundering, the settlers made it a practice to remind them that if their livestock losses were too great or if they were pushed too hard, the white men would ban together with weapons and stand up against the Paiutes and Navajo until they destroyed them. The Indians seemed to respect this unknown possibility and it made life a little easier for the settlers. Easier did not necessarily mean safer for the townspeople. Every member of the community knew that they needed to be careful in their travels, working in their fields and even at their homes. Nothing was taken for granted—especially safety.

Chapter Fourteen
"Me Want Biscuit!"

After seven years of unrelenting hardships, Jane and Charles were finally released from their assignment in Bluff. On March 4th, 1888, as the quarterly conference of the Church came to a close in the San Juan Valley, the Waltons, along with 20 other families, were called to join the newly established Blue Mountain Mission encompassing the Montezuma area. The same families who had worked to establish a settlement in the area a year earlier were now assigned to live there permanently.

Again, organizing a town government and assigning church responsibilities were the first priorities for the new settlers. F. I. Jones was named as the new bishop, and Charles Walton was chosen as one of his counselors along with Mons Peterson. These men would need to leave their families and homes in Bluff immediately and make their way to the Blue Mountain region to dig canals, build fences, establish patterns of freight, and plant more crops. While this new home was only 40 miles away to the north, it could easily have been hundreds. Although leaving Bluff was a welcomed change for Jane and Charles, it meant they would once again be starting over. The very thought of leaving friends and loved ones behind was very difficult since they had invested so much of themselves into making the town successful.

Charles and his son Charlie were the first to leave for Montezuma in order to ready things for the family who would later join them. Charlie was now a 20 year-old man and would be relied on to carry many responsibilities in building the new community. A week after the call to go to Montezuma, Charles and son walked out of their door in Bluff for the last time. Because of the late winter snows, travel was slow and difficult. In fact, it was deceptively dangerous as Bluff's elevation was lower and temperatures were much warmer than Montezuma's mountain location. Travelers could be caught unprepared for the journey. After several days of travel, the two men found themselves trudging very slowly through deep snow. They pushed and pulled their wagons and finally decided to leave them behind until spring. For several more days, father and son used their horses to break a trail through the waist-deep snow in order to continue their journey.

More men joined the father and son shortly after the two arrived in Montezuma. The men's first order of business was to make an accounting of the crops that had been left behind the previous year. The men became concerned when the cowboy they had entrusted to guard the provisions was nowhere to be found. Not only was the cowboy missing, but so was most of the bounty. The previous summer's work and the grain intended to give the settlers a head start on planting and surviving in Montezuma was now gone.

Back in Bluff, several of the men's wives decided to make the journey from Bluff to the Blue Mountain valley to surprise their husbands. A perfect spring morning dawned over the cliffs of Bluff as the women loaded a wagon and headed north. With cheerful smiles they waved goodbye to their town. The smiles, however, began to fade as the women reached the foot of the Blue Mountains and found themselves surrounded by deep snowdrifts and dangerous, icy conditions. To make matters worse, a heavy snow began to fall. Eventually, the snow became so deep that it was level with the stomach of the horse pulling the wagon and the animal refused to go any further. Unable to turn the wagon around and retreat, the women decided to unhitch the horse. They let a woman and her 2-year-old child ride, while the other women walked behind on the freshly broken trail. After a short distance, the horse stopped again and refused to walk any further. The women were trapped, and the weather was not letting up. Knowing that nightfall was descending on them, the women took turns carrying the child and tried to walk the remainder of the way. Exhausted and facing hypothermia, the women were becoming disoriented and confused. They sat down on a fallen log and began to pray.

Whether it was divine intervention or sheer luck, thankfully a cowboy from the L.C. Ranch, traveling in the opposite direction, came along on a buckboard wagon. When the man saw the women's condition, he immediately stopped and offered help. The cowboy pulled the supplies he was hauling off his wagon to lighten the load and then took the weary and freezing women on to Montezuma to their unsuspecting husbands.

As Spring approached, the men in Montezuma worked hard to clear the roads, and word was finally sent to Bluff that the

Montezuma mountain pass was clear. The families could begin migrating as quickly as they could tie up loose ends. Charles left Charlie in charge of affairs in Montezuma while he made the journey back to Bluff to bring his family north. For Jane, this move meant loading up all the family's possessions again and herding unruly livestock. The possibility of encountering unfriendly Indians along the way was an ever-present threat. In an arrangement made by the Church, personal properties were transferred, and homes were sold. Charles was able to sell his house and lot in Bluff to Bishop Neilson for $85 in "in-store pay" and $75 in cash. With the cash in his pocket, he, Jane, and their daughters, pushed their livestock and belongings toward Montezuma.

Once settled in North Montezuma, the new town leaders decided to rename the area. Folks began discussing several names that might be suitable, but local church leaders proposed that the area be called, "Antioch" after a biblical city spoken of in the New Testament. The name had special meaning in the Christian world because it was believed to be the first place that the term, "Christian," was uttered. The name, however, didn't sit well with Charlie, who had just finished reading a book about the life of Thomas Jefferson. Charlie liked the name of Jefferson's home, Monticello. He boldly convinced his mother and father that his idea for the new city's name was better than the other suggestions, and Jane and Charles joined Charlie in a clever whispering campaign. Soon, the townsfolk began to talk about naming the community Monticello, rather than Antioch. The Waltons handled this effort so subtly that when the community and church leaders met to make the name official, they seemed to forget their original intentions. Charlie made the motion to name the town Monticello, and his motion was quickly seconded by Jane. The vote was passed unanimously, and the name of Monticello was adopted.

The six families that settled Monticello that first year now needed to focus on building another town. Charles and the other men had mapped out the downtown area of the city the previous year. To ensure fairness, each of the six families drew a number from a hat to determine the order of choosing one of the 10-acre city lots as well as a 20-acre farming lot outside the city proper. Central to the lots, the settlers would construct a meetinghouse similar to the one that had been built in Bluff. It would serve as a school, government center and church. In a spirit of cooperation, the community began the daily work of building Monticello.

Weekends became a communal time as most of the families would travel up a canyon to a creek to wash clothes. The settlers tried to do chores together since greater numbers minimized the risk of calamity at the hands of the Indians. Once at the creek, folks would wash as quickly as possible, and then, swim, play and eat. On one particular occasion in June of 1888, while most of the townspeople were at the creek doing laundry, Bishop Jones excitedly announced that the August San Juan stake conference of the Church would be held in Monticello. Thrilled at the prospect of showing off their new settlement, the townspeople doubled their efforts to finish the community meetinghouse in time for the conference. Charles committed that for every two logs he harvested for his own cabin he would cut one additional log for the church meetinghouse. Charles would cut the logs and Jane would peel them. Together, they would evaluate the quality of the lumber and make sure that the very best logs were delivered to the meetinghouse. By the end of April, the Waltons were living in their new cabin and planting gardens and crops. The area surrounding Monticello proved to be a striking contrast to Bluff. The soil was richer, and the Blue Mountains provided adequate wildlife for dinner tables and the rivers and streams were filled with rainbow and brook trout.

By the time the conference started in August, the meetinghouse had been constructed complete with wood shingles on the roof and lumber benches fastened to the floor. Nearly 100 visitors attended the Monticello conference that year, each carrying their own bedroll and needed supplies for the several days event. Church members came from Bluff, Mancos, and Moab to attend the four-day meeting. At the conclusion of the conference, President Francis Hammond of the San Juan Stake published a letter in the Desert News describing the condition of the San Juan Mission in the Blue Mountains, "The new settlement is doing well. We have some 320 acres fenced with good wire fence, and about 100 acres planted with wheat, oats, barley, corn, and lucerne. All looking well when I last saw them. We have two dairy farms at this point, one on South Montezuma owned by William Adams and sons and another at Dodge Point owned and managed by Bishop Nelson, sons, and sons-in-law. The product of the two dairies per day is about 120 pounds of cheese of the finest quality. A few houses are completed and, a great many have logs cut and drying ready for hauling and putting up after harvest. Some, however, are living in tents, some in their own wagon boxes, others in the shanties."

Back in Bluff, problems with the Indians mounted as the United States government attempted to carve out segments of land for the exclusive use and habitation of the Native Americans. Financial enticements were offered to the Indians to settle the land swaps, which often resulted in a relatively inequitable trade for the natives. These land transactions were conducted for the purpose of satisfying the Indians and protecting the homesteader's interest. Many of the Southern Utes felt the land belonged to the tribe and petitioned the government for all of it, lock, stock and barrel. This notion was vigorously protested at every government level by the leadership in Bluff. The United States government proposed Indian reservation treaties that would give the Native Americans lands in exchange for land taken by white men. These treaties were readily accepted by some tribes and fought by others. The treaties would often involve the government purchasing land or providing financial buyouts, which were quickly taken but then later would become a source of litigation. If a white man's land was included in a treaty decision, the land was de-valued by the government to the extent that the settlers felt they were being cheated by their own. To minimize this concern, the government worked with President Hammond and other church leaders to summarize the Latter-day Saint position in Bluff. As discussions around the treaties continued, most of the people who resided in Bluff felt their best interests were being overlooked, prompting Bluff resident Jens Nielson to exclaim: "The Mormons are not anxious to leave their homes, but quite the reverse. The commission did not have time to visit Bluff, so they asked President Hammond to make an estimate of our claims and improvements and to place it at as low a figure as possible, promising to double it in their report, and to see that we received a fair remuneration for our trouble in moving. The estimate was given at one-third the actual cost; the commission cut it down two-thirds more in their report, thus allowing us about eleven cents on the dollar for our property. Our canal is not a failure, but on the contrary it has carried water to our farms and gardens every year since its completion. That we are squatters is partly true but only because the government has refused to survey the land and let us enter and secure title to our claims."

At that same time, President Hammond received a letter from his daughter who was living in Bluff. She said, "For some time past, the Southern Utes have gathered in the town nightly and engaged in singing and dancing. They have also indulged in a good deal of shooting, though no one has been hurt as yet. They have never been known to be so saucy and are angry because the government has not fulfilled the treaty obligations and given to them the San Juan County. They want the white people to move out of the county, and because they have not done so are almost on the verge of war. In fact, the feeling is so intense that if any rash person should engage in a quarrel, or do anything to offer a pretext, a massacre of the white population would follow. The Navajos are taking part. Red Jacket, the principal Southern Ute Chief under Ignacio is at Bluff City with about 250 braves."

The Indian troubles weren't confined to Bluff but extended to Monticello as well. One summer day, as Charles was away cutting timber, Jane went outside their cabin to hoe the garden. As she worked, she became aware of a horse galloping up behind her. She spun around to see a surly Paiute Indian approaching the cabin. In the distance she could also see several Paiute warriors sitting motionless on their horses, watching every move she and the Indian made. Jane recognized the Paiute as the infamous Chief Posey, the subject of many legends and terrifying stories.

Posey arrogantly dismounted his horse and in forceful, yet broken English said, "Squaw! Me hungry! Gimme biscuits!" Jane's mind began racing. She knew she could not run from him. The thought came to her mind that she should not show any fear. So, without speaking, she turned to her garden and continued her hoeing, hoping Posey would just leave. Posey stood, watching and waiting. After a moment, Jane realized he was not going to leave until she fed him. Growing tired of Jane's stalling, Posey again demanded, "Me want biscuits!" Finally, with as much confidence as she could muster, she said, "Posey, I'll fix you something to eat when I finish hoeing this garden." She was hoping she could stall for time until Charles came home. Jane was also remembering her earlier encounter with a Paiute at her cabin in Bluff, and she knew she needed to stay outdoors where perhaps someone traveling by might see her.

Posey grew impatient and pulled his Winchester rifle from his saddle scabbard and pointed it at her. "Me want biscuit now!" he shouted. Jane's pioneer fearlessness unleashed and, without thinking, she raised her hoe, and as hard as she could, smacked Posey right between the eyes. The blow to Posey's forehead made a noticeable pinging sound as the metal struck his brow. The Indian fell at Jane's feet in a crumpled heap and lay there as if he were dead. For a moment, Jane thought she had killed him. She resisted the urge to run into her cabin and lock the door. Instead, she somehow remained calm and returned to her hoeing as she tried to gather her scattered thoughts. Through the corner of her eye, Jane could see the distant warriors straighten up on their horses as they watched the scene unfold before their eyes. She realized they were staying put, perhaps as stunned as she was. While Posey lay on the ground and Jane continued her hoeing, time seemed to stand still. Suddenly, The Walton's pet dog could be heard growling as it bolted around the corner of the cabin. Chief Posey struggled to stand and staggered to his horse As he attempted to clamber up onto the horse's back, the dog grabbed the back of man's britches and locked them in his jaws. Posey gave his horse a forceful smack with the reins and galloped away leaving the back of his trousers in the faithful dog's mouth. Jane straightened up from her hoeing and watched Posey and his warriors hastily ride off past the river wash below the homestead into the dense cover. She breathed a deep sigh of relief and patted the dog on the head saying, "Good dog." She then headed toward the cabin as the dog continued his growling while ripping and tearing the remaining remnant of his victory.

As word of Jane's incident with Posey spread, the community, including Charles, became deeply concerned about possible Indian retaliations. The men began watching the community very closely for the next couple of days, sure that Posey and his clan would return for revenge. Some of the townspeople were angry with Jane for taking such a strong stand against the feared Indian. Others marveled at her courage. All, however, wished she had just given him what he had wanted and had let him go on his way. But, as the summer rolled into autumn, Chief Posey mysteriously stayed away from the town and the settlers focused on harvesting their crops in preparation for winter.

One fall afternoon as Charles was out harvesting the wheat fields and Jane was alone at home cooking cornbread, the door of the cabin slowly creaked open. Jane turned to see an old hat perched on the end of a stick jutting through the door opening. Seconds later Chief Posey poked his head through the door. "Squaw," he said softly, "me no mad, me want biscuit." Jane and her prior nemesis stood for a moment facing each other across the small cabin room. Jane smiled and said, "I'm not mad either Posey, but you'll have to wait until I finish cooking this cornbread before you eat." Satisfied, Posey glanced around the room to make sure there was no garden hoe, then squatted in the corner and waited patiently.

Not another word was spoken between the two, yet each was aware they had come to a certain understanding. Soon, the cornbread came out of the oven and Posey's belly was full. Jane anxiously watched Posey walk out of the cabin and pick up an axe near a woodpile. Starting to panic, Jane tried to collect her thoughts when she turned to see Posey chopping an armful of wood. He then carried the wood back into the cabin and carefully placed it next to the fireplace. Without saying a word, he left the cabin, mounted his horse and rode away. Jane understood the two had developed a newfound respect for each other. She no longer concerned herself with the stories of his murdering rampages and she certainly didn't fear him as she had feared his legends. She respected Posey because he respected her.

Posey had come from an entirely different culture than Jane. To an Indian warrior, women were akin to possessions. They were servants who had the responsibility to cook and clean and to care for the children while the men provided food and protection. Many times, Indian men criticized the white man for doing womanly chores like cutting wood for fireplaces and cooking. When Indians observed white men opening a door for a woman or helping one into a wagon, they were baffled. It seemed as though they came from two separate worlds to this space in the San Juan that they shared.

Jane put her experience with Chief Posey's threatening behavior behind her and the Indian grew puzzled by her non-judgmental and unthreatened attitude toward him. Some people thought that Posey assigned some mystical powers over Jane that manifest itself in the way she stood up to him and refused to be intimidated by him. Whatever the reason, Posey and Jane enjoyed a peculiar relationship that seemed hinged by their uncharacteristic differences.

Chapter Fifteen
A Snowy Solar Eclipse

In their first year at the base of the Blue Mountains, the six families who had been called to settle the area were able to harvest enough hay to feed their livestock through the winter and enough grain and vegetables to fill their own stomachs. Fall brought the rain that was so badly needed in the summer, but it came as a torrential, troublemaking homewrecker, streaming through the cabin roofs that acted like a sieve. Tubs, pans and buckets were quickly filled and dumped like water being bailed from a sinking ship. Children hunkered down in the driest spots of the cabins while the adults did all they could to keep the bedding and clothing dry. It wasn't long before the rain turned to sleet as temperatures dropped.

As October turned to November, the settlers prepared to observe Thanksgiving. The autumn holiday always heralded a time of deep reflection and gratitude, and after the townsfolk had worked tirelessly to bring in crops and stock barns with feed for livestock, their heartfelt prayers were heard. It had been a year full of hard work, struggle, and sacrifice, and their survival now rested upon the fruits of their labor. As the winter weeks creeped up, the families of Monticello began to prepare for Christmas. Like Thanksgiving and many other special occasions during that first year, Christmas of 1888 became a tender memory in the minds of those first families. The financial condition of the settlers was lean, and gifts were not bounteous, yet each family did their best to make sure the holiday was special. Although it was Christmas morning, the livestock needed feeding, cows needed milking and eggs needed gathering

Everyone in the Walton family gladly pitched in to complete the chores while Jane cooked a special breakfast for her family. The family also took time to reflect on and read the biblical account of the birth of the Christ child. New snow had fallen the night before, so several men fashioned a V-shaped contraption out of fence posts and attached it behind a team of horses. The apparatus was dragged up and down the streets of the community to clear a pathway for traveling. Unable to resist the freshly fallen snow, the children raced to complete their chores so they could play on home-built sleighs and toboggans. Some of the older children in the community saddled up a horse or two and pulled the younger children on a long rope across the snow. At noon the families within the new community gathered together at one of the cabins for a potluck luncheon. Everyone brought more food than was needed, and the serving table overflowed. Mary Adams served grape tarts, and everyone enjoyed the feast of Jane's special rolls, breads and butter. The meal consisted of mashed potatoes and stewed chicken with gravy. The desserts were especially appreciated, and everyone marveled at Mary Jones' beautiful white frosted cake. The real fun began after the meal when William Adams danced and sang an Irish song while swinging his Shillelagh:

"Oh! an Irishman's heart is as stout as shillelagh,
    It beats with delight to chase sorrow and woe;
When the piper plays up, then it dances gaily,
    And thumps with a whack to leather a foe."

Adams had carried his Shillelagh across the ocean and over the plains. The Irish-made walking stick was also a formidable weapon in the 1800s and many countrymen from the United Kingdom became as proficient in its use as the swordsmen of Japan. A strike from a Shillelagh could disable or even kill a man.

Emma Hyde broke the group into hysterics as she entered the room draped in a lace window curtain and performed a Highland Fling while her husband sang, "I'm not as young as I used to be." The performance brought tears of joy to Jane's face as she watched her Scottish traditional dance performed by her hilarious friend and neighbor. The "fling" was an old dance from Scotland, performed by soldiers who were returning from a victorious battle. Emma was no male Scottish warrior but, she could not have acted the part better. Frederick Jones played his mouth harp while everyone danced in the confined quarters of the home. Later someone announced a square dance and, "Old Peko is Hitched to the Cowhide," and "Anyone Want to Go Home?" was called out with enthusiasm. Christmas 1888 was unforgettable, and the settlers of Monticello cherished the memory for many years.

On New Year's Day 1889, the families of Monticello were again enjoying a community lunch, this time at the Jones' home when, "an uneasy quiet fell over the group as the room became darker and darker and the snow at the window took on an unusual hue." Parley

Butt ran outside, looked up at the sky and shouted, "It's a total eclipse of the sun!" With joy restored, the party continued and, the group pledged their New Year's resolutions.

January brought blizzards that piled mountainous snowdrifts high enough to cover fence posts and reach the roofs of the cabins, and the six families of Monticello began to feel isolated. For nearly two months there had been no visitors to Monticello. There were no doctors, no mail service and no passersby. On one cold winter day, while the children were at school, two of the boys saw a couple of horsemen riding over the hills south of town. So rare was this sighting that school was closed so the children could run home and report the news. The townspeople excitedly ran to greet the travelers and then fed them a warm meal while firing dozens of questions about current events and the news from other communities.

During that first winter, the cold temperatures, coupled with drifting snow, became such a problem that school was discontinued in the meetinghouse. So much time had been spent stocking the wood-burning stove in order to keep the room warm for the children, that the settlers opted to move the classes to the cellar of the Rogerson home where the confined quarters were much easier to heat. For a time, the nine students from the Monticello School enjoyed the change of pace in the new environment. Three nights per week, the adults also gathered for school where they too learned reading, arithmetic and geography under the tutelage of William Adams. Sunday services were also held in various homes throughout the tiny community in order to preserve the dwindling supply of firewood. Each family enjoyed the opportunity they had to host the church meetings and they took pride in getting their cabin ready for the congregation. To make the visit memorable, each homeowner strived to have a small edible treat that would delight those who attended.

During the long dark winter, the settlers continued the daily doldrums of caring for their livestock and keeping their cabins warm until the short days and long nights of winter were over. As the winter months came to a close, the town welcomed March and April with enthusiasm. There had been one death during that first winter, Eliza Peterson had died of pneumonia; but the sadness of her death was replaced with the joyful birth of two healthy babies.

Life in Monticello remained anything but predictable. The settlers consistently endured confrontations with hostile Indians, outlaws and the unpredictable cowboys. Often, drunken and disorderly wranglers would come into town looking for trouble. Cowboys were the hardest group for Jane to understand because at times they were very kind and polite, while at other times they came through town acting very unruly and threatening. The settlers had learned various tactics for dealing with the Indians but a method for dealing with cowboys was yet to be discovered.

The settlers continued to prescribe to Brigham Young's philosophy to feed, rather than fight the Indians. Some of the settlers disagreed and felt that feeding the Indians only enabled laziness and a sense of entitlement. Regardless, Jane and her family made sure that no individual, Indian or otherwise, ever passed by their home hungry and the Walton family refused to make a dinner guest chop wood before being fed. If a wanderer insisted on following the custom of chopping wood for a meal, Jane graciously accepted it. If they didn't, she fed them, nonetheless.

In both Bluff and Monticello, the settlers began to notice that the Indians were becoming more aggressive as more white families moved into the area, homesteading land that was otherwise used by the Indians. As conflicts between whites and Indians escalated in the San Juan region, fear among settlers in the area began to spread.

By mid 1889, assaults and threats by the Indians became daily occurrences. Negotiations between the Indians and the government over reservation land and land available for white men to homestead had slowed. This prompted San Juan Stake President Hammond to write to Governor Arthur L. Thomas on October 15, 1889: "The San Juan settlers are really in danger because of the restless condition of the Indians, they are regarding the white men as trespassers.... It has cost the settlers from $3,000 to $4,000 a year to feed the Indians and make presents to them in order to maintain friendly relations with them. The government should either open this region for settlement again, and assist the settlers to reclaim this deserted land, or else take it for reservation purposes. In the event of [it] being held as a reservation, I would suggest that a committee of three be appointed with power to act, who should repair at once to this region, look over the country the Utes are to leave and the country they are to occupy, that they may see and understand fully what the government is to give and what it is to receive, and determine the value of the settlers claims. The settlers cannot improve the land in consequence of its being withdrawn…settle this vexed question once and for all."

While the people of San Juan pled for government intervention, they also continued to give gifts and food to the Indians in order to maintain peace. The delicate balance for land was discussed in Salt Lake City and Washington, while settlers continued to build up the towns they had agreed to settle.

Jane and Charles lived more than 100 miles from the nearest railroad and much of their business and church related travel required days in a saddle or on the seat of a buggy or wagon.

Most of the meetings they were required to attend were in Moab, approximately 50 miles to the north, and Bluff, another 50 miles to the south. Travel to Mancos, Colorado was an eighty-mile trek to the east. While Charles insisted that Jane never make the trip to any of these communities alone, often times she did so out of necessity while she continued to serve as the stake Relief Society president. As president of the organization in the San Juan Valley, Jane's ecclesiastic responsibility carried her throughout the area from Moab to New Mexico, and from Mancos and Cortez in Colorado to Bluff in order to care for the women of the church. In a buggy or wagon, in heat or cold, she seldom, if ever, failed in the duties of her assignment. Jane was a woman of integrity and grit and she had an infectious love for life. Whenever she found women complaining about a certain principle of the gospel such as polygamy, her advice to them was simply, "If you find yourself in disagreement, do not say 'I don't believe,' just say, 'I don't understand.'"

Jane and Charles both had church responsibilities in Monticello. Charles was the clerk to the San Juan Stake, requiring his attendance at many meetings in many different locations. It took him a full day to ride a saddle horse to Bluff, or two days in a buggy. If either was hauling freight in a wagon, the trip was much longer. Travel to Mancos was a three- or four-day trip. Fortunately, the Waltons had regular stopping points along the way where they could get water and camp for the night. There was an unwritten rule among the settlers that meals were served, and beds were provided to any traveler that happened by.

In 1890, Charles and Jane made the long journey north to visit Jane's family in Bountiful and attended general conference in Salt Lake City. Instead of the impossible route taken on their initial journey to Bluff, travelers used a much simpler route that took them north to Moab and then further north to Salt Lake City. In order to make the trip, the Waltons had to give up three months of time and the income earned from missing an entire season of threshing. It would take almost ten days to make the trip from Monticello to Bountiful and along the way, they stopped and helped several other travelers who had broken down or needed help locating missing livestock. They were pleased to be able to help others and were grateful they didn't need help on this particular journey. Just as folks were expected to feed travelers, equal responsibility fell on travelers to help other travelers in need. When horses wandered off, all joined the search. When a wagon wheel broke and couldn't be fixed on site, a passerby would offer assistance. Life on the frontier was demanding and a handshake or a personal pledge to do a task was akin to making a legal contract. People kept their word, and their word was their bond.

In those early years, currency was rare, and most people traded labor and goods. Folks worked for each other on jobs that required more than one man and paid their debts with cash, commodities, or with personal labor. When someone needed money, they could borrow from others. People saved everything with the idea that it might become useful at a later date. Men, women and children all learned essential skills. Even children could saddle a horse or hitch a team. Everyone in the family needed to know how to wash clothes. Water needed to be carried from a stream or irrigation ditch into homes where it was heated on a stove and then poured into a tub or basin. The clothing was hand washed by running it back and forth on a piece of corrugated metal. It was then rinsed clean and hung out to dry in the fresh mountain air. If the clothing needed ironing, a flat iron was heated on the stove and was usually heavy enough to press out all the wrinkles. Fuel for stoves and for heating homes was cut and stored each fall. There was usually much more stacked wood than was needed. Running out of firewood in the winter would be disastrous. It was a mistake that usually only happened once.

In 1889, Mons Peterson built a general store in Monticello and it quickly became known as, "Monses Store." Staples such as grains, sugar, coffee, chewing tobacco and other necessities were stocked in the log store that was covered with a dirt roof. The front door was perforated with bullet holes fired by the drunken cowboys who would periodically ride into town. One day, to be a little more original than the rest, a local cowboy rode his horse through the door of the store. He took hold of the end of a bolt of calico cloth, wrapped it around the horn of his saddle, and rode out to the street on a full gallop, unwinding the bolt as he sped up the road. Some Ute squaws were in town that day and when they saw the cowboy with the fabric, they ran him down and each cut off enough of the textile to make a dress. The cowboy and his partners had come in from Carlisle Ranch, drunk and disorderly. The men shot up the town and broke up quite a number of Mons Peterson's store goods. Unfortunately, the vandalism was commonplace, and it was becoming more than Mons could afford.

By the opening days of January 1891, the community of Monticello had grown by leaps and bounds. Hundreds of people walked the streets and farmed the land. Drunken cowboys gambled nightly and instigated fights regularly. Trouble with the Indians had become a never ending problem and some settlers continued to question the wisdom behind Jane's relationship with Posey. They were sure the murderer's true character would one-day surface resulting in Jane, or other townspeople, being hurt. There were others in the community, however, who thought the relationship was positive and provided the town with a level of protection from any violence Posey or his warriors might inflict. Either way, life in the west was anything but quiet and mundane. To prosper on the western frontier was a precarious lifestyle of shifting and evolving challenges.

Chapter Sixteen
Ruffian

Twelve miles southwest of Monticello, a hardened cowboy named Tom Roach watched the sun rise over the Blue Mountain Range as he sat in the saddle of one of his two white horses. In the distance, he could see the outline of several other cowboys he had been working with from the Carlisle Ranch. They were employees of Carlisle while Roach was an independent ranch hand. Three years earlier he and, "old man Carlisle," had had a disagreement that led to Roach's firing. The incident had begun when one day, Carlisle was sitting on a fence near Roach. Roach had been riding his horse in circles inside the Carlisle Ranch corrals, swinging his lariat. Ignoring Carlisle's repeated demands to "quit swinging the fool rope," Roach jokingly raced his horse toward Carlisle and rope-whipped him across the shoulder so hard that it knocked Carlisle to the ground. Stunned, Carlisle fired Roach on the spot and ordered him off his ranch. Carlisle received many complaints from other ranch hands about the firing and he ultimately rescinded the action. He offered Roach $10 per month if he would agree to continue working for him. But Roach was too proud to accept the offer, and he resorted to branding maverick cattle for himself and helping out the Carlisle boys from time to time.

After more than three weeks of herding cattle on the upper ranges of the Blue Mountains, Roach and the Carlisle cowboys were more than ready to take a few days off. These cowboys were a tough and brazen group of men who, by many accounts in the San Juan, were outlaws from Texas and the Midwest. The group included marauders such as Butch Cassidy, Mont Butler, Tom McCarty, Matt Warner and other members of the notorious Robbers Roost gang. Roach's attitude and ornery disposition helped him fit in with the wild bunch.

Tom Roach was a tough, mean man who was prone to cause trouble. He had had confrontations and arrests from as far away as Ogden, some 350 miles north of Monticello to Green River, Utah, 100 miles north of Monticello. He was well known in the Green River area and had once told a bartender named Thomas Larsen that he'd come to Utah from Iowa, where he'd left a wife and son. Larsen recalled that Roach was an excellent shot with a pistol and was also a man who knew that gunfighters did not play fair. Roach once heard about a cowboy who had been shot by a man using the cowboy's own revolver. Roach not only pledged such a thing would never happen to him but, rigged his revolver so that only he knew how to fire it. He did this by removing the "jumping dog"— the small lever that rotated the revolving cylinder of a pistol with each trigger pull. Roach became an expert at pulling the trigger with his second finger while he rotated the cylinder with his first finger. According to Larsen, this had saved Tom's life more than once.

Larsen had a favorite story he swore Roach personally had told him. According to Larsen, Roach had stolen a flag off a wagon that the local madam and her working girls were riding in on the 4th of July parade in Green River. The madam became furious, and when Roach returned the flag with a broken stick, she threatened to kill him if only she had a gun. Roach handed her his revolver and she immediately pointed it at him and pulled the trigger, but nothing happened. She pulled the trigger three more times before Roach wrestled the gun from her hands, leaving no question in Roach's mind that she meant business.

Larsen also remembered a time when Tom Roach had been playing cards with a "half-breed" and known killer named, Indian Joe. When the card game didn't go his way, Joe had become unruly, provoking Roach to whip him across the head with his pistol. Not wanting to do more than get the man's attention, a somewhat penitent Roach washed his unconscious victim's wound. When Joe awoke, he said, "You hit me, didn't you Roach?" Roach replied, "You were getting unruly Joe and I had to." This made Indian Joe angry and he reached for his gun saying, "You will never hit another man." Before Indian Joe's gun cleared its holster, Tom Roach drew his revolver and, in self-defense, shot Joe through the heart, killing him instantly. Grand County Deputy Sheriff Tom Trout had been standing in front of Roach during the argument and, although stunned, replied, "The bullet singed my whiskers as it went past my face."

Not only was Roach well known in the mountains and bars throughout the region, but he also had a reputation in Monticello as a troublemaker, drinker and womanizer, even though he lived in town with his "other" wife, Millie. The Roach's lived across the street from Monticello's meetinghouse, and while most people in town stayed away from Tom Roach, they enjoyed Millie's company, a girl who was quiet and friendly. Some thought Millie was the wife from Iowa. Others swore she wasn't. Nobody really dared ask either one of them.

Tipping his cowboy hat to block the morning sun, Tom Roach sat tall in his saddle and spotted a young calf that had wandered away from its mother. Instantly, he dug his spurs into the side of his horse and raced toward the calf. The crashing sound of his powerful quarter horse broke the silence of the morning and immediately grabbed the attention of the wayward calf. The calf bellowed loudly and turned abruptly as the experienced rider whistled and whooped while swinging his braided rope over his head. The calf froze in its tracks, and then bolted to the side of its mother. Roach loved the solitary life of a cowboy, roaming the beautiful countryside day after day. He would say it was his way of "communin' with God." Roach was different than the farmers in the area—he didn't feel the need to attend formal church meetings. He had attended church a few times with Millie, when they were first married, but nowadays he just didn't favor such structured spirituality. He felt closer to God in the mountains than he ever did sitting on a hard church pew. In the mountains, Tom Roach could quietly show compassion by helping a calf across a swollen river or through a deep ravine. But Roach would never allow anyone to see this side of him. To him, sensitivity was a weakness and fatal character flaw. According to Tom, if others knew about a person's weakness, they'd take advantage of it.

After his initial check of the herd, Roach met up with the other cowboys back at their camp for breakfast and a cup of coffee. With the cattle nearby, the cowboys enjoyed the cool morning air and the smell of pork rind and biscuits cooking in the pan. Coffee always seemed better sipped from an old tin cup, especially one tempered with years of use and little rinsing. After a hearty breakfast, courtesy of old man Carlisle, Tom tied his bedroll to the back of his saddle, turned to the other cowboys and said, "It's Brigham's big party tonight boys." It was July 24th, and throughout the day, celebrations that had begun under the direction of the first Territorial Governor, Brigham Young, would be commemorating the 1847 pioneer's entry into Utah. As the men broke camp, Roach boasted, "I'm gonna teach those pretty Mormon girls how to dance tonight." With that, the men saddled up and got to work doing what cowboys do best.

By mid-afternoon, Tom Roach had collected thirteen dollars in his pocket and was heading toward Monticello. The Carlisle Ranch paid their cowboys well, and Roach, a freelancer, was one of the more experienced and well-paid ranch hands. Millie was looking forward to getting that money to offset some of the couple's mounting bills. She knew that the time between Carlisle placing the money in Tom's hands and her husband's ride home, was a critical interlude. Tom had a tendency to spend his wages unwisely, usually on whiskey. This day, the lure of the saloon would find Roach and his dusty, saddle-tramp peers drinking up their hard-earned cash. As the afternoon waned into evening, Millie thought to herself, "It's happened again."

Chapter Seventeen
A Fateful Night

As Jane quietly sang the final verse of her favorite hymn, she noticed her oldest daughter Magnolia standing in the doorway of the kitchen. Magnolia asked her mother if there were anything she could do to help with preparations for the July 24th celebration that evening. Sensing there was more to her query, Jane asked her if there was something she would like to talk about. Magnolia replied with a simple, "no," prompting Jane to point toward a large bowl of bread dough. Taking the cue from her mother's motioning hand, Magnolia picked up the dough and began kneading it with her hands, which, like her mother's, were pioneer strong and capable, built from years of work on the frontier. As she kneaded the dough, Magnolia smiled and thought of the handsome young man she would soon spend the majority of her evening—with dancing and talking. Although seven years her senior, 29-year-old John Bailey was a hard-working immigrant from England who lived away from his parents' home and was already building his own cabin. He was the kind of man she could envision herself marrying and deep down inside she knew that they would soon approach her parents to talk about their plans for marriage, perhaps even tonight.

While Jane and Magnolia continued to prepare food for the celebration, 22-year-old Leona gathered a basketful of potatoes from the cellar. Leona, like her sister and mother, was already an accomplished homemaker and a very good cook who enjoyed creating new dishes. She loved to quilt and found pleasure in her association with the other young women of Monticello. Unlike her sister Magnolia, however, Leona wasn't settling on any particular young man in the valley, at least not now.

Charlie was also looking forward to the dance and a chance to play the violin in his father's stead during a few of the breaks. Some of the folks in town had been overheard to say that music came naturally to the Walton boy. But Charlie, now 23, attributed his skill to the long hours he had invested in learning to play an instrument and improving his technique. Most often, practicing came late at night, by candlelight, when his father had time to teach him a few notes or share his techniques. Not only did Charlie play the violin, but he also played the coronet and the mouth harp. From time to time, he would take one of his instruments into the field to practice. Whether on the mountain while timbering, or in the fields as he was herding livestock, Charlie could be found practicing his music to the accolades of cattle, squirrels and birds.

Charlie was in a hurry. This particular morning, he was responsible for slaughtering one of the co-op owned cows for the town barbecue. He had enlisted the help of his longtime friend, Frank Adams. As he finished his chores, Charlie yelled to his father that he was grabbing the horse and buckboard wagon and heading over to Frank's house. Charles Sr. cautioned his son to have the cow cut and hanging on the spit by noon. No one loved a slice of tenderloin beef fresh off the spit more than Charlie. He had been planning on this celebratory day for some time and had been feeding one particular cow with a little extra grain. He hitched the old mare to his flat bottom wagon and moments later, with a stir of dust, he headed out of the Walton gate.

Franklin Jacob Adams answered simply by the name of Frank, the son of William and Evelyn Adams. Charlie and Frank were fairly close in age and they enjoyed one another's company immensely. Charlie thought that Frank was one of the best cattlemen he'd worked with and the pair acted more like brothers than friends. Charlie was a seasoned hunter and enjoyed teaching Frank how to stalk wild game. The two had spent a great deal of time that first winter in Monticello trapping beaver, fox, coyote and bobcat together. When properly cured, the tanned furs brought a handsome income, supplementing many of the expenses of life in the San Juan. When time permitted, the two friends would spend time fishing, but mostly, they just plain worked together, and hard. They had accompanied their fathers during that first exploratory year in Monticello and worked side by side throughout each day. Working together grew their friendship into a brotherhood. During that first summer in Monticello, the young men had dug ditches on the upper farming territory and had become valuable work hands to their fathers, the original settlers of the area.

Frank Adams was a good shot with a rifle and often borrowed the Walton's 45-70 rifle to hunt deer and elk. The 45-70 long barreled rifle was a product of the Springfield Arms company and it was favored by the military for many years. It was a single shot, black powder weapon, but unlike its predecessor, it didn't require pouring powder and dropping a ball. The bullets and gunpowder were contained in a newly engineered single container called a cartridge, one of the giant leaps in the technology of weaponry. The rifle was nicknamed the "Trapdoor," because of a flapping apparatus at the top of the trigger assembly that would pop open for loading the single bullet. The marksman behind the gun sights had to be very precise when firing the weapon, as the billowing black powder smoke would take seconds to clear from view. Because of the smoke, animals being hunted could see the location of the shot and would flee the area if missed. Thus, missing the target was not an option for the shooter of the Trapdoor. The entire rifle was nearly the same length as a standing man—52 inches long and weighed just over eight pounds. When it struck its target, the Trapdoor was as lethal as any weapon made, and it usually knocked its intended target violently to the ground. Charles Sr. often remarked, "When Frank Adams takes a shot at a deer it usually drops dead in its tracks. He is the best shot of anyone I know, and he can clean a deer slicker than a whistle." Frank considered the comments to be quite a compliment and he took pride in his marksmanship.

Frank was an impulsive and quick-thinking young man. As Charlie rounded the corner to pick Frank up for the slaughtering, he noticed Frank waiting at the end of the lane, near his cabin. Leaning against a fence, Frank was focused on something he held on his thigh. The morning sun bounced a reflection off a twelve-inch steel blade and Charlie saw that Frank was sharpening his prize Bowie knife. Without missing a beat, Frank jumped onto the slowing buckboard with the exposed blade of the knife in one hand and the wet stone he was using to sharpen the blade in the other. He spit on the stone and slowly moved the blade back and forth, refining the edge for the job ahead. Without looking up, he greeted Charlie and commented that it was nice day for a dinner and dance. Charlie laughed at Frank's attempt to be proper and cautioned him about sharpening a knife blade on the bouncing old wagon. "Frank, you'll cut your finger clean off," he cautioned. And with that warning, the two men headed off to process a 1,200-pound steer.

From a distance, Chief Posey and his braves watched throughout the day as the settlers prepared for the big celebration. Seeing the abundance of food and smelling the aroma wafting through the trees, caused the spectators' stomachs to complain and grumble. They knew that the settlers would feed them if they were to go into town, but they were always cautious since the territorial marshal and the United States Army were continually pursuing them. As Posey sat atop his horse, he was startled by the noise of a wagon lumbering by. He turned in time to see Charlie Walton and Frank Adams returning from butchering the cow. Charlie halted the wagon as Posey approached. Although the Chief and Charlie's mother were friends, he still felt uneasy as the Indians came closer. With a smile, Posey recognized and greeted the younger Walton. Charlie dismounted the wagon seat and after sizing up Posey and his warriors, he generously cut off enough meat to feed the small band. With smiling nods of approval, the Paiutes thanked Charlie and Frank for their generosity and immediately took the meat and began to prepare it over their small fire. The men shook hands, and Charlie and Frank waved goodbye and started again toward town.

As the two rode away, Charlie told Frank about an experience he had the previous winter with some of the same Paiutes. He said he had been on the Blue Mountain the previous fall with Nielsen and some other men from the town and was rounding up the last bit of livestock from the summer range. Snow had begun to fall lightly, but quickly became a blinding blizzard. Soon the men found themselves cold, wet, hungry and lost. After wandering back and forth for most of the day, they came across a group of Indians. At first, the cowboys didn't know what kind of reception they would receive, but soon found the Indians to be very friendly. The Indians escorted the men into their camp, helped them warm-up, and offered a meal of game stew that they had been cooking over a fire. Before the men could eat, they were handed a dull axe. The Indians then made each man chop an armload of wood before they would feed them, all but Charlie. Instead, they fed him first and wouldn't allow him to cut any of the wood. Charlie ended his story quoting one of the Indians: "Charlie's family always feeds us first, without having to cut wood. The other white men make us work first before we eat. This is difficult because we are already weak from hunger."

At about one-thirty in the afternoon, Charlie and Frank pulled up to the town square with the anticipated quartered beef. Jane Walton and a group of women had been waiting for them and within minutes, the beef quarters were sizzling on the fire spits and grills. The beef's aroma signaled the celebration was about to begin. From every direction, families began to pour into the town's center, each bearing their own contribution to the meal with delicious cakes, fruits, vegetables and fresh-baked rolls. Everything seemed to be coming together for a wonderful celebration as the once seedling settlement of six families now numbered in the hundreds. With just hours to go before the anticipated meal, most of the town, along with many visitors, headed over to the corrals for the start of the always popular rodeo. All ages participated in the event, including children who chased a greased piglet around the corral trying to catch and lay claim to it. Children also rode bucking sheep, imitating the adult bareback riders. The women's barrel racing was a favorite sport and competed for attention with the men's steer wrestling. But the preferred event was the wild mustang and bull riding competition where the cowboys competed against the fiercest of livestock, hoping to stay onboard for eight seconds. Most importantly, they hoped to avoid getting injured.

After the rodeo, everyone gathered at the town's meetinghouse where tables and chairs filled every space. Bishop Frederic I. Jones offered a blessing on the food. Jones was the senior member of the settlers and the ecclesiastical leader. In his prayer, he acknowledged the blessings and protection the town had enjoyed. His tone and words touched everyone, and his love for the people and the community was evident. He was, in return, loved by them. Bishop Jones had long been an icon in Monticello, serving as its first bishop. He watched out for the youth of the community and always tried to protect them from the antics of drunken or cruel cowboys, having once been a victim himself. It had been a cool fall evening when he had encountered a few drunken cowboys. Without warning, the rowdy men had drawn their pistols and shot into the air. With cruel grins, they had ordered the bishop to dance. Jones had complied and danced while the men shot six-shooters at his feet.

When the bishop ended his prayer, the community gathered around the food and plates began to fill. By evening, no one was left hungry and everyone was ready for a night of dancing. Samuel Cox and Charles E. Walton, Sr., along with members of their shoestring band, were tasked with playing the music for the dance. Each performer earned four dollars for his contribution of time and talent that night. Everyone's favorite "caller", John E. Rogerson, was designated to call out the instructions during the square dances.

By 8 pm, the musicians began playing songs for the young people and continued through the remaining daylight hours. While the youngsters danced, adults cleared and cleaned the tables. Chairs were moved into groups for socializing, and young men and women cautiously made their way to the dance floor. Some young men politely asked a girl to dance, while others hung back and watched, hoping to garner courage. Several of the adults took turns "calling" for the group dances. From time to time, Charles and Samuel slipped a slow dance into the mix for those young men and women brave enough to dance as a couple. It was a beautiful night, and everyone seemed to be having a wonderful time.

As the young people of Monticello danced, Charles caught Jane's eye and directed it toward the dance floor where Magnolia gracefully swayed in the arms of John Bailey. Magnolia and John had danced nearly every dance together that night and seemed inseparable during the breaks. Jane thought of how often John Bailey had come by their home and how he had always walked Magnolia home from church on Sunday afternoons. It seemed that Magnolia and the Bailey boy were getting to be more than just friends.

By around 9 pm, the children had tired of the festivities and the fiddlers prepared for the next group of dancers. Soon, the sun dipped below the tops of the mountains and July's heat dissipated, darkness covered the landscape. The youth dance came to a close, and the adults gathered in the meeting hall for their turn. Jane loved to dance, and would dance with anyone, but she always looked forward to young Charlie filling in for his father on the fiddle so husband and wife could dance together. To accommodate the small dance floor, it was necessary for every member of the community to be assigned a "dance number". This meant that couples and individuals would dance every other song depending on the number they were assigned. Those with odd numbers danced first, followed by those holding even numbers. This made it possible for everyone to dance all night long and yet have enough room on the floor to enjoy it. The dance was in full swing by 11 pm when Tom Roach and a few of the drunken Carlisle cowboys rode into town with their usual "whiskey'd-up" whooping and hollering.

Roach entered the make-shift dancehall and demanded that Frank Hyde, the dance floor manager for the night, give him a number so that he could dance. Hyde kindly obliged and explained the rules to Roach, informing him that those with even numbers could only go on the dance floor when it was time for an even-numbered dance. Roach tore the ticket from Hyde's hand, stepped onto the floor and began dancing. John Rogerson was calling a square dance and Roach "clapped" his way into a quadrille, frustrating Peter Bailey who had to relinquish his dance partner as was the custom. Peter was angry, knowing that the polite thing for Roach to do was to wait until the next dance. Unfortunately, Tom Roach was full of liquor and was long past being polite, arguably a trait that was not part of his makeup to begin with. Between the even numbered dances, Roach would leave the dance hall and go outside where he would get a drink from a hidden bottle of whiskey. Frank Adams had noticed Roach drinking from the concealed container but turned the other way since he too had been drinking. As each dance break was announced, Roach grew more intoxicated and more belligerent. As the clock passed the midnight hour, he finished off his bottle of whiskey and returned to the dance only to discover that he had missed his turn. According to the rules, Roach would have to wait until the next even-numbered dance began. Drunk and angry, Tom grabbed an unwilling partner named Eliza Holyoak and pushed his way into one of the quadrilles, ordering Peter Bailey and his partner off. Bailey refused and an argument and scuffle broke out. While Bailey and Roach squared off, dance manager Frank Hyde approached Roach and again explained the simple rules, reminding him that he would need to wait until the next dance. Roach was very inebriated and squared off with Hyde. He angrily pulled out his knife and swung it across Hyde's face, cutting him deeply from his ear to the tip of his chin. Frank Hyde fell to the ground in agony and many folks started running for the door. Some ran to help Hyde, and others ran to grab their guns, sensing that things might get worse.

During the raucous, Frank Adams had slipped out a window of the meetinghouse and headed toward the Walton cabin with the intent of obtaining Charles' 45-70 rifle from above the fireplace. Inside the dance hall, Roach quickly shoved his knife back into his boot. His long-time friend, Bill McCord, approached him in an attempt to calm him down. His efforts only enraged Roach who instinctively pulled his revolver from its holster and pointed it at McCord, ordering him to "shut-up". McCord began to plead with Roach to put the gun down. Roach would not comply. Just then a few men came forward to help McCord subdue Roach. Roach swiftly pointed his gun at them and told them to stay put.

"No one has injured you, Tom," McCord told him. "They've done with you the same as with everybody else. They just wanted to be fair and you ought to be fair with them." he said.

"Shut up or I'll kill you!" yelled Roach.

McCord plead, "Tom, for your own sake and for the sake of everyone else, go home to Millie and let the dance go on in peace."

McCord slowly extended his open hands to Roach and looked into his eyes as he waited for Tom's response. To everyone's horror, Tom Roach pulled the trigger on his revolver with his second finger, rotating the cylinder with his first finger, and fired a lethal bullet into McCord's chest. McCord was dead before his body hit the ground.

"Don't anybody move, or I'll shoot you too," Roach bellowed to the stunned crowd. Like a wild animal that had been cornered, Roach's eyes shifted, right to left, as he tried to analyze his options. At that moment, Jane, being true to her character, stepped toward Roach and confronted him with firmness and confidence, "Tom Roach, you put that gun away." Jane had known Tom for many years and had been in his home, visiting his wife Millie. She was the kind of person who accepted people for who they were capable of being, not just who they were. Tom Roach respected Jane Walton and he seemed to be confused by her demand. Just then, Frank Adams staggered through the door of the meetinghouse armed with the Walton's rifle. As Jane was trying to reason with Roach, the young man raised the rifle to his shoulder and aimed. Roach instinctively ducked to escape Frank's aim. With perfect precision, Roach swung his revolver, and while his first and second fingers moved across the weapon in perfect harmony, a shot rang out.

The sound of the gunshot rang through the building and everyone dropped to the floor. Time seemed to move slowly—second by second. Crawling along the floor as fast as they could, townsfolk sought cover from the gunfire. When the commotion ended, Jane was left standing. She took a few stumbling steps and, with confusion and sorrow in her eyes, grabbed her chest and said, "Oh Roach, you've hurt me." Charlie rushed to his mother and she collapsed in his arms.

Amid the confusion, Tom Roach fled the building and galloped away on his horse. Many in the room took off after him, while others attended to Jane. Outside, a group of townspeople surrounded the lifeless body of Bill McCord. Charles, Charlie, and John Bailey, carefully picked up the mortally wounded wife, mother and lifelong companion, and carried her home with hopes of saving her life. Jane was placed on the floor in front of the fireplace—her blood dripping and staining the wooden floor of the cabin she had helped build. Charles Sr., Charlie, Magnolia, John Bailey, and Leona knelt at her side.

At forty-five years of age, Jane closed her eyes for the last time. The memory of that long-ago dream in which Jane's father appeared to her, came to Charles' mind. Just as her dream had predicted, Jane was taken in her 45th year.

Chapter Eighteen
The Investigation

    The day after the murders, Charles busied himself with his chores—consistent with his life on the frontier. He hoped work might help keep his mind off the events of the previous day. As he headed for the barn, he paused to look toward the kitchen window, then toward the well. For many years, the outline of Jane washing dishes at the sink or drawing water from the well gave him the extra push he needed to continue on. Jane had worked hard to establish the homestead and she was immensely proud of it. Charles knew she would want him to carry on with his life as they had known it. With Jane gone though, Charles wondered not so much if he could endure life without her, but rather, if he wanted to.
    Friends and neighbors began streaming in and out of the Walton home, viewing Jane's body and offering condolences to the family. Almost fittingly, Jane lay in a pine coffin that was carved from trees

cut from her beloved Blue Mountains. Only those who lived near the Waltons would have the opportunity to view her before the funeral. Sadly, Jane would be buried before her mother or siblings would learn of her death. Her headstone, ordered through Monses Store, would cost five dollars and ten cents. The Hammonds, Lymans and Bishop Nielsen and his wife spent the majority of the day with the Walton family as a number of friends and family from Bluff made the trip northward. The news of Jane's death traveled quickly throughout the San Juan and plans were made to bury her on the following day, Sunday July 26th.

Following the deaths of Jane and Bill, Mary Jones, the new Relief Society president in Monticello was contacted by the Carlisle Ranch and given a message for the Waltons. She delivered the message to Charles saying, "Charles, Mr. Carlisle contacted me and said that none of his men were responsible for Mrs. Walton's death and he would like to give you this pair of white silk stockings in which to bury her." Mary indicated that she had the stockings in her wagon if Charles would like them, to which the grieving widower said, "Thank you Sister Jones. Please tell Mr. Carlisle we appreciate the offer and would prefer not to take the stockings."

Nothing more was said about the shooting or what led up to it. As far as the Waltons were concerned, what was done was done, and revisiting the issue wouldn't change that. Throughout the day, many offered words of comfort to Charles and his children, which they deeply appreciated, but they knew their life in the San Juan would never be the same. Focusing on the funeral plans helped Charles make it through the day and he hoped the weather would cooperate for the funeral on Sunday. Unfortunately, it didn't. The simple service was held anyway on that stormy sabbath day, and later that evening, Charles took out his journal that he had so faithfully kept over the years and wrote, "Funeral services were held at two o'clock p.m. and my beloved wife was laid away until the resurrection day." Jane McKechnie Walton would become the first person buried in the Monticello Cemetery.

Jane had crossed the Atlantic Ocean and walked the American plains. She had survived the harrowing epic at the Hole in the Rock, and she had stood up to threatening Indians on the frontier. She had endured all these trials, only to have her life taken away by a wayward bullet as she courageously tried to act as a peacemaker for the town and people she loved.

* * * * * *

From the day of the murders, Sheriff Willard Butt had been working on the investigation. As the first paid employee of San Juan County, Butt made one hundred dollars per year, independent of fees, for his services. For that abundant salary there were great expectations, and he had proven in the past that he was a dutiful public servant. Like the Waltons, Sheriff Butt had also been part of the original Hole in the Rock expedition and he was one of the most colorful men in San Juan County. He had been a long-time friend of the Waltons, having forged a foothold in the frontier alongside them. Butt was a hearty, no-nonsense lawman, but was also very friendly and the first to open his doors to strangers, cowboys and even the local Indians. He loved a practical joke and was well known for his wit and humor. These days, however, the sheriff was is no mood for jokes. His mind was consumed with bringing Jane Walton's and Bill McCord's murderer to justice. He immediately began interviewing witnesses and gathering evidence related to the events leading up to the shooting. Everyone he talked to agreed that Tom Roach was in the middle of all the disruption and fracas. Many recounted similar stories of the moments leading up to Roach pulling his knife and slicing open the face of Frank Hyde. Even Hyde, now tightly bandaged up, was able to talk personally with the Sheriff. There were so many witnesses who saw Roach's unprovoked and violent attack on Hyde that the sheriff didn't worry about his chances of getting a jury to find Roach guilty of the violent assault.

With the Hyde incident neatly tied up, Sheriff Butt then focused his interviews on the shooting of Bill McCord. One by one, the witnesses to the murder said that McCord had valiantly tried to calm Roach down. Even Nora Jones, the person who clearly had the best view of the shooting said, "When McCord persisted, Roach shot him on the spot." Not one witness, including the cowboys from the Carlisle Ranch, disagreed with Jones's description. Many of those cowboys admitted that even Roach, himself, knew he had finally gone too far, which was evidenced in the way he fled the area as soon as the gunshots rang out.

Lucinda Nielson Hyde, daughter of Jens Nielson and wife to Frank Hyde, also witnessed the events. She explained that Bill McCord and Tom Roach were "great pals, but neither would take a suggestion from the other," she said. "Tom Roach could sing and entertain and dance, and was very popular, but when he had a drink, he was a rascal." She told the sheriff that she witnessed Frank being slashed and McCord being shot by Roach.

Now, armed with two warrants for Thomas Roach's arrest, the sheriff concentrated Jane's murder. As the days turned into weeks, some evidence surfaced that Roach may have hidden himself inside Bob Hott's barn for a few days immediately following the shootings. Another lead came from Ben Perkins who said Millie Roach had contacted him asking for help in moving some of her possessions to the town of Thompson. Millie boarded a train shortly after and left for an unknown destination. Unfortunately, Perkins didn't give this information to the sheriff until after Millie had left town, and the sheriff was never able to question her regarding any contact she may have had with Tom.

As Butt's investigation continued, several facts became clear. First, there had been two people in the meetinghouse with loaded firearms, Tom Roach and Frank Adams. Second, there were as many versions of how Jane died, as there were witnesses. Most echoed the testimony of Lucinda Hyde who stated she was unsure who shot Jane Walton. "There was shooting all around and McCord and Sister Walton fell," she said. "After the smoke cleared, I watched as Tom Roach's wife ran to, and cried over Jane's body. Roach had fled the scene."

Townsfolk were convinced it was Tom Roach's bullet that took the life of Jane Walton since Jane declared in her own words, "Oh Roach, you've hurt me," immediately after the shot rang out. Everyone knew that Roach had been a violent troublemaker and criminal. He had violently attacked Hyde with his knife and then shot his cowboy associate Bill McCord at point blank range. To Sheriff Butt, it was an open and shut case. Based on his investigative experience, and testimony from witnesses, the sheriff was able to get another arrest warrant issued for Thomas Roach. Now he needed to find the fugitive.

One blustery morning during the investigation, the feared Indian Chief William Posey, accompanied by a large number of his finest warriors, ceremoniously rode into town. The Paiute warriors had shaved the hair from their heads as a symbol of sorrow, respect, and love for Jane, the customary way of grieving in the Ute and Paiute nations. Sitting tall upon their horses, they solemnly rode in a line, acknowledging no one, as they made their way toward the offices of Sheriff Willard Butt.

Sheriff Butt was well known to Posey and his warriors. He was not their friend, nor were the warriors a friend of the law. Butt and the United States Army had pursued Posey for years, hoping to either kill him on the trail or bring him to justice for his many crimes. As Posey and his dozens of warriors halted their horses in front of the Sheriff's office, a subtle cloud of dust settled. The sight was impressive. The horses snorted and whinnied as they pawed at the ground. Posey dismounted while the warriors remained in their saddles, each instinctively kept an eye out for any sign of trouble. Posey walked cautiously toward the sheriff's office as the door opened and Sheriff Butt emerged.

A calculating and wise man, Butt quickly summarized that he was heavily outgunned. For a fleeting moment he thought of the accolades he would receive by taking William Posey into custody. With wisdom on his side, Butt realized that today would not be the day to do it. With his Winchester lever-action rifle cradled in his left arm, and his right hand rested on the weapon's trigger, Butt stepped onto the porch and greeted the chief. "What can I do for you Posey?" he asked. Chief Posey stood tall and looked as if he was preparing to salute when he said, "Me want to help find Roach." The sheriff was astonished at the outlaw Indian's offer. "Jane Walton friend. You need posse and we go," replied Posey in the best English he could muster. And with that, the deal was made between the government and the criminal. The renegade outlaw Indian chief was made the leader of a murder posse under the direction of Sheriff Willard Butt who later acknowledged, "I needed a posse, and they were the best darn trackers in the land, plus they were available. There was no way

I was going to affect an arrest on that renegade with all his warriors standing by and frankly, it just seemed to make a lot of good sense."

There was no special swearing in ceremony or signing of documents—no training and no badges to wear. With the deal struck, Posey and his warriors hastily rode out of Monticello in pursuit of the felonious murderer, Tom Roach. The cloud of dust from the hooves of their racing horses could be seen for over a mile, as the posse headed toward the Blue Mountains where Roach had spent so many years wrangling cattle. Both the predator and the prey were now relying on their experience in the outdoors to either elude or capture. As the sheriff watched the non-traditional posse ride out of town, he wondered if he had done the right thing. Butt knew if Posey found Tom Roach first, the murderer would probably never be returned alive. Thinking about the loss of two of the city's most loved citizens, the sheriff saddled up and set about to bring the murderer to justice—dead or alive. Although it was Saturday, Sheriff Butt contacted the local magistrate and swore out a warrant for the arrest of Thomas Roach in the San Juan Courts for the murder of Bill McCord and Jane Walton. Sheriff Butt knew he had a lot of work to get done before a trial could be held, that is, if Roach survived an extradition at the hands of an Indian posse. Like the sheriff, few people in Monticello thought they would ever see Tom Roach alive again after watching Chief Posey and his warriors take up his pursuit.

Many days passed and Sheriff Butt continued to wait anxiously for the Paiute posse to return with the prisoner. He had heard that members of Posey's posse had been seen in the region, including Posey himself, but he never received a report indicating what may or may not have occurred during the hunt. Days turned into months and then years and Roach was never seen again.

Posey never disclosed whether Roach had been located and killed by him and his men, or whether he had once again escaped the law and gotten away.

Chapter Nineteen
Afterword

Autumn in Utah can be filled with unpredictable weather. Rainstorms can change to sleet and then snow in a matter of minutes, especially when traveling over higher elevations. It was early morning, and my police car was slipping and sliding as it approached the tiny Utah community of Monticello.

"I hope you don't mind Palmer. I'll only be a moment," I said. Palmer DePaulis and I worked together in the Attorney General's Office. He was the former mayor of Salt Lake City and we were friends. He smiled and nodded as he sipped his coffee. We'd been driving for nearly six hours and needed to stop and stretch our legs anyway. For more than 100 miles, I'd been telling him about my great-great-grandmother and my research into her life as part of my new passion in genealogy. I explained that her name was Jane McKechnie Walton, and from the time I was a boy, I had heard stories about her heroic journey through the Hole in the Rock and her untimely death in 1891. The mystery about her death had been in the family for over 100 years.

I was almost shouting to be heard above the incessant screeching of the worn-out windshield wipers as I said, "I heard she was buried here in Monticello. If you'll give me one minute, I want to ask someone at the local chamber of commerce if they can help me find her grave." Palmer was a member of the Catholic Church and had a personal appreciation for genealogy— courtesy of a gift he received from the Church of Jesus Christ of Latter-day Saints. A member of the Church's First Presidency, Gordon B. Hinckley, had surprised the mayor with a copy of his own Italian family history, dating back hundreds of years.

Palmer accepted my invitation to come inside with me. When we entered the Monticello Chamber of Commerce building, we were greeted by a very elderly woman sitting behind the counter. She seemed frail but very kind. Knowing we didn't have much time to spare, I simply asked, "I wonder if you could tell me anything about a woman named Jane Walton. She lived here about 100 years ago?" With a stunned look on her face, the woman straightened up a bit, pointed her crooked finger at my nose and asked, "Are you family of Mrs. Walton?"

"Yes I am. I heard she might be buried in the Monticello cemetery," I said.

A sweet, almost grateful smile came across the woman's face. "Young man, we're not related, but I have the journal of Jane Walton's husband," she said. "My grandfather gave it to me when I was just a girl. He asked me to hold on to it and take good care of it, because a family member of Mrs. Walton would come looking for it someday. Would you like it?"

Her words sent shivers down my spine and I turned to look at Palmer who stood wide-eyed and motionless. I couldn't believe what I had just heard. I eagerly told her I would love to have the journal. I turned toward Palmer again. Without speaking a word, we both knew that something very special had just occurred.

The kindly woman told me that my great-great-grandmother was murdered on Utah's statehood holiday in 1891. Incredibly, she added, "Just this year the town had a celebration and part of the town play was a reenactment of her murder." She then scrawled a simple map on a piece of paper showing me how to get to the city cemetery and where I would find her grave. Suddenly, the meeting Palmer and I were rushing to didn't seem very important, and Palmer wasn't pushing me to hurry. By the time we walked out of the building and toward the car, the storm had lightened up, but still, a rather dreary rain sprinkled down.

Following the shaky, hand-written directions to the cemetery, we made our way down a dirt road and through the small metal gates of the Monticello City Cemetery. Focused on her directions and looking for Jane's tombstone, I had completely forgotten about the rain. I drove along with my window down—my head leaning out like a dog. I didn't notice the rain pelting my face and kept replaying the words the old woman said as we were leaving her office: "Jane Walton was the first person buried in the Monticello Cemetery. She has a story worth telling."

Within a few minutes, the rain miraculously cleared up and the fresh smell of wet grass filled the air. When I located the grave, I found myself weeping as I knelt down to read the name of this ancestor I had never known. After the short cemetery visit, I returned to meet the old woman and retrieve the journal that had remained hidden from our family for more than a century.

Weeks later, I sat down to read the fragile pages. I spent several days captivated by the words written in my great-great-grandfather's beautiful penmanship. The experience was emotional, spiritual and thrilling. For a brief moment I felt as though I had reached through the veils of heaven and embraced my long deceased ancestors. I could feel their presence as I read his words. When I came to the page dated July 24, 1891, I was astounded to read:

"Friday the 24th. Cloudy. We celebrated the 24th and had a good time. At night I played for the dance and got 4 dollars. Between 12 and 1 o'clock, Tom Roach started a row, killed a cowboy and Jane was accidentally shot by Frank Adams, a drunken Mormon boy, with my own gun, a 45-70 caliber. The ball passed clean through her body just under the arms killing her instantly.

Saturday 25, Stormy. Things were got ready to bury Jane."

* * * * * *

As a boy, I would hunt the mountains around Monticello with my grandfather and cousins. It was the highlight of my year to gather on the Blue Mountain where we'd camp and listen to stories of the "good ole' days". I knew the country well. What I didn't know, and what no member of my family could give me, was a definitive answer to who had killed Jane McKechnie Walton. I started looking into her murder in 1985. It would take nearly ten years and an old journal to solve the mystery.

As a former investigator I couldn't help but analyze the case. I could have called it good, but I was just too curious how the investigation evolved. Utah journalist, Tim Gurrister said it best when he read Jan's story. "A murder trial more than one hundred years after the fact, faces many obstacles. Chief among them: it is impossible," he said. "Every witness is long dead, leaving memories rusty at best; evidence is likely lost, records deteriorated. No doubt though, it is a lively trial, with room enough, like the San Juan Valley itself, for the diversity of large, strong personalities and varied glimpses of lifestyle in the broad range of characters likely to take the stand."

I found myself asking, "How was the investigation of Jane's murder conducted, and what would the criminal investigation of this case look like today?" Multiple accounts still persist as to what happened the night Jane was killed. Murder charges were never filed against Franklin Jacob Adams, but the warrant for Roach's arrest still remains on the books of the San Juan County Court.

It seems clear, Sheriff Butt had his hands full. We don't know much about his background and training, but it is safe to say that he was understaffed. As the first and only paid employee of the new community, he probably self-funded any equipment he used in the performance of his duties. That equipment probably only consisted of a gun. There were no back-up officers available to him. If he needed help, it could take days or weeks to receive. There is no mention of a jail having been built at that time and there certainly weren't evidence lockers to hold any items that may have been collected at the crime scene. The sheriff would have known every member of his tiny town and may have even been in the vicinity of the celebration when the shots rang out. If so, was he armed? Did he try to intercede? During the early days of settling the west, policing in America was in its infancy. As the sole law enforcement officer in the community, the task of investigating a murder must have posed many unique challenges for Sheriff Butt. There is always a great deal of confusion at any murder scene. Most people run from the scene to safety, while others run toward it, trying to help. Managing the crime scene alone, must have been nearly impossible for the sheriff. His first order of business seems to have been to interview a room full of witnesses. Foremost in my mind is the importance of gathering evidence from the crime scene. In this case, an investigative eye could have evaluated the physical evidence at the scene and assessed how it aligned with other forms of evidence such as the location of Roach, Adams and Jane. The physical evidence could have then been analyzed against such findings as: eye-witness accounts, forensic evidence, such as shell casings, and the bullets fired. Circumstantial evidence would also have played a powerful role in the investigation. By combining each form of evidence, a conclusion could have been made about Jane's murder, and the person responsible for her death.

Surviving a gunshot wound in the old west of the 1800's was nearly impossible. If a bullet didn't immediately kill the victim, the loss of blood, internal damage and infection would. Most cowboys in that era carried a six-round .36 or .44 caliber revolver. Either weapon was lethal, especially when the victim was a small-framed individual like Jane. Bullets were made of lead and would often pass right through the body unless the projectile struck a bone. If Jane had been shot by a 45-70 rifle, the round would have undoubtedly passed through her body. Rifle rounds travel at a much higher speed, and with much more force than revolver rounds. This creates an interesting forensic challenge. Was the bullet that killed Jane ever recovered? If it did pass through her, it likely became embedded in one of the pine logs that made up the walls of the dancehall. What direction did the bullet come from? Obviously, there was no coroner available to the sheriff. It appears Jane's wound was never examined. Her body was immediately carried to her home and then prepared for the mourners. Most likely, Jane's body was buried rather quicky since there was no way to embalm it.

Witnesses testified that Tom Roach shot Jane, but eyewitnesses can have varying stories. In fact, eye-witness account can be the least reliable form of evidence in a criminal investigation. People can be influenced in many different ways when they witness something as horrific as a homicide. Their thoughts, feelings and emotions can skew their memory and perception of what really occurred. This situation, coupled with a person's personal bias, can create a real accuracy problem. In the minds of most of the partygoers, Roach was a troublemaker. If anyone could have been capable of murder, it was him. In fact, he'd murdered his friend only moments earlier. What isn't clear is how Sheriff Butt analyzed the various accounts.

Charles knew all along who killed his wife. He knew that only a bullet from his own powerful rifle could have passed completely through her body. However, he realized the killing was an accident and he did not want to incriminate Frank. He told Sheriff Butt, "Sheriff, Frank Adams is a good boy, and he needs to tell the truth. He also needs to know that we Waltons don't hold no grudges for accidents. Please try to spare the boy any embarrassment. Frankly, I don't think either of those men would purposely have hurt Jane in any way."

Sheriff Butt appears to have handled the matter on his own—understanding Frank had good intentions and Jane's murder was both an accident and an act of defense. If Tom Roach had been killed by the Indian posse, it seems the sheriff felt he got what he deserved. As it turned out, it was a 100-year-old journal, preserved for so many years, that solved the crime.

* * * * * *

Several years after obtaining my great-great-grandfather's journal, my wife and I made a trip to Monticello. I wanted to show her Jane's grave and also try to get a bit more information about the other individuals in this story. I was told to visit a woman in the community charged with keeping the town's history. I called her as we drove, and she graciously invited us to her home for a visit. When we arrived, she showed us shelf after shelf of books lining her living room walls, containing historical records of the San Juan Valley. She told us that she knew every person in the area and the history of their families. I showed her my ancestor's journal and explained how I had come to possess it. When I told her about the old woman at the chamber of commerce building, she said, "I don't know who you are referring to. There has never been an old woman working there".

* * * * * *

Franklin Jacob Adams became a successful cattle rancher, starting his business at age 16. He established a mine in San Juan County and named it Jacob's Chair. Many years later, it would be used to gather uranium for the atomic bomb. His first wife Minnie died after two years of marriage, at age 20. Frank inscribed: "God's finger touched her, and she slept," on her Bluff cemetery tombstone. He married Lucy Bronson in 1915 and they enjoyed a happy life until his death at age 62. Frank drowned on October 5, 1940 while trying to cross the rain-swollen White Creek after a thunderstorm. In the article, "Cattleman of the Canyons" by Neal Lambert, Adams proclaimed moments before entering the river, "Ah, hell you c'n cross this." He then charged his horse into the torrential runoff and disappeared. The horse was later found dead a few hundred yards down river and four days later, searchers found the battered and broken remains of Adams lodged behind a rock in the stream. His tombstone reads, "Died in White Canyon By A Flash Flood: His Life Shall Be My Guiding Star."

Joanna Murray Bee (Jane's aunt) married George Thomson in 1853, and he died only a few years later. She then married Arthur Welchman in 1860. She remained active in the Latter-day Saint church and died on January 14, 1913 in Grover, Wyoming.

Richard John Moxey Bee (Jane's uncle) and Georgina McKechnie Bee (Jane's sister) had moved to Woodruff, Utah during the initial years of that settlement. They later moved to Georgetown, Idaho. The two had a large family and remained active in the Latter-day Saint Church for the remainder of their lives. Georgina died on

February 21, 1912 in Idaho and Richard Bee died shortly after on July 18, 1912.

Jean (aka Jane) Tinto Bee McKechnie Hatch (Jane's mother) continued to live in northern Utah the remainder of her life. Her American husband, Ira Stearns Hatch died on September 30, 1869, leaving Jean alone to raise their youngest children. She remained faithful in the Latter-day Saint Church and lived in the same home in Bountiful until her death on August 9, 1915.

Chief William Posey was eventually arrested by U.S. Marshals but the charges against him were never formalized. He was extradited by train from the San Juan Valley to a Salt Lake City magistrate in 1915, though the arrest and trip ended up being more of a vacation than punishment. Upon arrival, he was hosted almost as visiting royalty in a peace overture, including being treated to his first and only silent movie, which according to his escorts, frightened him. He was later released and returned to San Juan with no charges filed. Posey never did bend to the white man's authority and he died alone, "off-reservation" in 1923 of a gunshot wound from his final skirmish. He was arguably, "the last openly defiant American Indian." U.S. Marshal Jesse Ray Ward took possession of Posey's remains and buried him in an unmarked grave. The chief's resting place, however, was located and exhumed at least twice by people wanting photographs with the corpse.

Thomas "Tom" Roach may have survived the Posey Posse, although most people think he didn't. There have been no documented accounts of Roach surviving. His wife, Millie, quickly left the Monticello region for an unknown destination. On June 15th,

1896 the murder warrant for Thomas Roach's arrest was re-issued in San Juan County. This may suggest that the sheriff was unsure whether Roach was dead or alive.

Charles E. Walton, Sr. (Jane's husband) continued to live in Monticello after Jane's death. He was the first person called from San Juan County to serve as a full time missionary for the Latter-day Saint Church. The call came only two and a half years after Jane's death and he faithfully served in the Southern States Mission from 1894 through 1896. After his mission, he moved to Logan, Utah in 1904 where he served for many years as a temple worker. Charles later married Ellen Ricks and they enjoyed a long and happy life. He died in Logan, Utah on December 14th, 1923.

Charles "Charlie" Walton Jr. (Jane's son) remained in Monticello after his mother's death. He married Emma Louise Hyde in 1896 in Monticello and the couple had five children. He was given the distinction of being the first postmaster of Monticello. His commission was made by U.S. President, Benjamin Harrison. He continued in that position (except for a period of eight years) until 1934 when he retired. During his eight-year hiatus from government service, Charles had joined his father in Logan, Utah where the two worked in a sugar factory. Charles Jr. served as the San Juan Country Treasurer from 1935 to 1939 and continued to serve in the Latter-day Saint church until his death on May 9th, 1947 in Monticello.

Leona Jane Walton (Jane's daughter) left Monticello a year after Jane's death. She married Francis Nielson, son of Jens and Kirsten Nielson, on November 30th, 1892 in the Logan Utah

Temple. They had nine children. Leona died in Salt Lake City on September 9th, 1942.

Magnolia Francis Walton (Jane's daughter) continued to live in Monticello after her mother Jane's death. On June 2nd, 1892, she married John Ezra Bailey. Magnolia became the mother of 7 children, one of which was Clifford Walton Bailey (author's grandfather). Magnolia died after a long illness on September 7th, 1918. Her husband, John, then married a mail order bride selected from an ad in the Montgomery Ward Catalog, named Lillie May Cox on November 6, 1919. Sadly, Lillie was not well received by the Bailey children.

Acknowledgements

Throughout my life, I've heard the stories of my great-great-grandmother, Jane McKechnie Walton. Her life story was somewhat vague and there was a great deal of mystery surrounding her death. Most of what I learned came from my grandfather, Clifford Walton Bailey. I could listen to him tell stories for hours and I cherished those tall tales. I can't think of them today without envisioning the flicker of a campfire while hunting or a gas lamp while sitting in his cabin at Strawberry Reservoir.

In those settings I learned who Jane really was. She was a woman of deep faith who gave everything she had for her beliefs. As a child she braved a transatlantic voyage and walked the American plains, mostly barefooted. She accepted church assignments without hesitation and always put God's will before her own. She taught her children the value of hard work, respect and resiliency and those characteristics have passed from generation to generation. Without those stories, I would never have become curious about Jane.

I've spent the last 40-years working in law enforcement in some capacity. I retired from police work in 2004 and started consulting and training police officers around the world on investigative techniques and the use of technology in crime-fighting. Along the way, I became friends with Tim Gurrister, a local crime reporter with the Ogden Standard Examiner newspaper. I dealt with Tim on a regular basis as he walked the halls of police headquarters trying to chase down a story. He was known for ferreting out information where none existed in other people's minds. As I put the story of Jane's life on paper, I asked Tim to give it a read. He was immediately captivated by Janes story and stated, "The European emigration and pioneer movement has rekindled in me a deeper sense of appreciation for those who sacrificed all to come to this area you call Zion." He continued by saying, "Jane's story is one of the most amazing stories never told. I cannot get away from the fact that not so very long ago taking a jaunt to say, Denver, or maybe Phoenix, wasn't just a long day-trip on asphalt in an air-conditioned car, but a gauntlet needing a group caravan where you slept with your rifle wondering if the Indians would scare away the wolves in the dark." I greatly appreciate the suggestions and contributions Tim made to this book.

The next person I shared Jane's story with was my friend and New York Times Best Selling Author Philip Carlo. I described her life and challenges as Phil and his wife Laura joined me for dinner in Miami. As I related Jane's harrowing experience with native Americans, Phil actually leapt to his feet and exclaimed, "Me Want Biscuit! – Mike, you gotta write this book!" Thankfully I was able to deliver a printed copy to Phil shortly before he died from ALS, commonly known as "Lou Gehrig's Disease". I thank him for the support he offered.

I want to acknowledge my amazing children for their ideas and critiques along the way. It is important that these histories are passed from parent to child, so they, too, can come to know about their ancestors are. I can see Jane's strength in them. And most importantly, I want to thank my beautiful wife and companion Bonnie. She has given hundreds upon hundreds of hours in reviewing, editing and cleaning up my words. The cover should have her name on it, but she won't allow me to do so. Anything good that I have accomplished in my life is because of her influence.

Finally, I express appreciation for the life of Jane McKechnie Walton, my great-great-grandmother. It has been wonderful getting to know her. I hope this book represents her accurately.

I learned much by examining my family history. It taught me who Jane was and who I am. It has since caused me to reflect on a scripture from the Bible which reads, "And he shall turn the heart of the fathers to the children and the heart of the children to their fathers, lest I come and smite the earth with a curse." – Malachi 4:6

Chapter Notes

Chapter One:
Jane McKechnie Walton was born: International Genealogical Index - British Isles, Film Number: 1239609, Page Number: 29, Reference number: 733.
Both of Jane's parents: Family Search Ancestral File, Church of Jesus Christ of Latter-day Saints. Spouse: John McKechnie (AFN: 22GK-T9) Family Marriage: 12 Jul 1844 St. Cuthberts, M-Lthn, Scotland.
Jane's father was a brass founder: Walton History by Pearl L. Walton.
John McKechnie joined the ranks: Family Search Ancestral File, Church of Jesus Christ of Latter-day Saints. Spouse: John McKechnie (AFN: 22GK-T9) Death: 3 January 1848, M-Lthn, Scotland.
George had been: Bee, Journal.
One day, while walking to work: Walton, Pearl
Perpetual Emigration: National Parks Service History.
February 21, 1850: Walton Family History.
…journey to America from Liverpool: North Atlantic Ship Passenger List.
It may not be on the mountain height: Hymns, #270.

Chapter Two:
An article in the London News: Illustrated London News.
Registered on the passenger list: North Atlantic Ship Passenger List.
Amidst the uncertainty of ocean travel: Davis.
Far more terrible was the fate: Davis.
In the 1850s the famous: Davis.
Later, the steamship Tempest: Davis.
Other sea disasters during the next twenty years: Davis.
One disaster involving church members, however: Devitry.
After several weeks at sea: Bee, Richard.

Chapter Three:
She was deeply grateful for: Ship's Master.
Twenty third Psalm: Holy Bible, King James.
Within a few days of Mrs. Hulme's death: Bee, Richard.
We are rocking in the bosom of the deep. Bee, Richard.
After eleven weeks at sea, The North Atlantic: Bee, Richard.

Chapter Four:
New Orleans seemed manageable: Wikipedia.
a good slave could be purchased for twenty-five dollars: Bee, Richard.
Richard was fortunate in securing employment: Bee, Richard.
While in St. Louis I witnessed the sale at public auction: Bee, Richard.
Wilford Woodruff wrote, "I have never: Church History, Chapter 25.
On June 8, 1852 Jean and her children: Howell, Thomas C. D.

Chapter Five:
Young's 1847 order said, "At five o'clock: Wagon Train Rules.
On Wednesday, June 9, 1852: Howell.
The men appeared to huddle together with the Indians: Condie.
Although the saints were singing of a "fallen race," the: Condie.

Chapter Six:
In the morning, after the cattle were all yoked: Hatch, Ira.
There were fresh graves all along the way for miles: Tanner, Rebecca.
A most un-soldierly looking lot they were: Kelley, William.
The brethren were very kind to us in this our affliction: Osborn, David.
It was a grand sight to see hundreds of them [buffalo]: Condie.
I marveled to myself how the pioneers could find their way: Condie.

Chapter Seven:
She was standing next to me and didn't recognize me: Bee, Richard.
to prohibit in the territories those twin relics of barbarism: Utah War.
A retreat was ordered and later, U.S. Army Captain: Utah War.
"We appeal to you as American citizens who: Utah War.
"PROCLAMATION ON THE REBELLION IN UTAH": Utah War.

Chapter Eight:
As the Civil War was raging: Utah War.
many were discouraged with the prospects of farming: Woodruff.
"we're going through and we're going to…: Walton Family History.

Chapter Nine:
In 1863 a Paiute man and his Mexican wife: Native Languages.
Having put the deadly plan in motion: Posey, The Last Indian War.

Chapter Ten:
Some of our party are of the opinion that a road could: Lyman.
"We've got another group going into the backcountry: Lyman.
I would like to leave my vote to President Smith: Nielsen, Jens.
"a bird could not fly over the route: Walton, Charles E. Sr.
"Before we left our homes we were told that the country: Rowley.
"Here is where a decision was made that has affected: Jones, Kumen.
"We will go on whether we can or not: Nielsen.
"The Spirit of God: Hymns.

Chapter Eleven:
A decision to send another scouting party: "Hole in the Rock".
On New Years Day the four walked into camp: "Hole in the Rock".
"Coming down the hole in the rock: Decker.
"The wagon of Joseph Stanford Smith was the last: Gaunt.

Chapter Twelve:
those that wish to move away were released: Walton Family History.
In March of 1887, a frustrated: Walton, Charles E. Sr. Journal.

Chapter Thirteen:
a conflict called, "The Pinhook Battle": Posey, The Last Indian War.
Toorah was the sister of Posey's best friend: Posey, The Last Indian War.

Chapter Fourteen:
Charlie like the name of Jefferson's home: Walton Family History.
The Mormons are not anxious to leave their homes: Nielsen, Jens.
For some time past the Southern Ute's have gathered: Hammond.
One summer day as Charlie was away: The Blue Mountain Shadows.

Chapter Fifteen:
Like Thanksgiving and many other special: Walton Family History.
On New Year's Day 1889 the families of: Walton Family History.
The real fun began after everyone had eaten: Walton Family History.
This prompted San Juan Stake President: Hammond.

Chapter Sixteen:
Three years earlier: Tom Roach, Cowboy and Fast Gun.
One of Larson's favorite stories: Tom Roach, Cowboy and Fast Gun.
Joe became unruly, provoking: Tom Roach, Cowboy and Fast Gun.

Chapter Eighteen:
"And should we die, before our journey's through: Hymns.
none of his men were responsible for Mrs. Walton's: Walton History.
Funeral services were held at two o'clock: Walton, C. E. Sr. Journal.
Tom Roach could sing and entertain and dance…

Bibliography

Allen, Stephen. *The Killing of Jane McKechnie Walton*, Blue Mountain Shadows, Summer 1992.
Bee, Jean Tinto Bee McKechnie Hatch. *Personal Journal*, Mike King custodian.
Bee, Richard John Moxie. *Life Sketch Written from Memory*, Mike King custodian.
Church History in the Fulness of Times, The Church of Jesus Christ of Latter-day Saints, 2003.
Condie, Gibson. *Reminiscences and diary*, 1865-1910, 33-35
Davis, C.L. Never Heard of Mysteries of the Atlantic Ferry. http://www.theshipslist.com/ships/Wrecks, 1900.
Davis, Harriet Jane Osborn, [Reminiscences], in Edith Parker Haddock and Dorothy Hardy Matthews, comp., *History of Bear Lake Pioneers* [1968], 172-73
Devitry-Smith, John. *The Wreck of the Julia Ann*, BYU Studies, 1989.
Gaunt, LaRene Porter. *Hole in the Rock*, Ensign, October 1995, 49.
Hammond, F.A. *The San Juan Settlers...*, Utah Enquirer 15 October 1889).
Hatch, Ira Stearns. *Personal Journal*, Mike King custodian.
Historic New Orleans Collection, Williams Research Center, New Orleans, LA www.hnoc.org
Holzapfel, Richard N. *The Civil War in Utah*, Utah History Encyclopedia, h ttp://www.media.utah.edu.
Howell, *Thomas C. D. Thomas Howell Company*, Mormon Pioneer Overland Travel, 1847–1868.
Huntsman, Orson Welcome, Diary, in Library of Congress, Collection of Mormon Diaries [1935-1938], reel 4, item 5, vol. 1, 1-2.
Hyde, Lucinda Nielson, Quote, Hole in the Rock website: http://trekholeintherock.blogspot.com/2010/01/walton-charles-eugene.html
Hymns. The Church of Jesus Christ of Latter-day Saints, 1985.
Illustrated London News. *The Departure*, July 6th 1850
Jones, Kumen. *Quotes Found in the book, "Hole in the Rock"* Utah History Atlas, 2000.
Jones, Mary. *History of Mary Jones*, History of Mary Jones, 1946, page 9.
Keller, Fred W. *Anecdote*, Blue Mountain Shadows, Summer 1992.
Kelley, William, *Journal*, LDS History Library
Lacy, Steve and Baker, Pearl. *Posey The Last Indian War*, Gibbs Smith, 2007.
Lyman, Albert R. *Indians and Outlaws, Settling of the San Juan Frontier*, Bookcraft, 1962.
Lyman, Platt D. *Quotes Found in the book, "Hole in the Rock"* Utah History Atlas, 2000.
Miller, David E. *Hole in the Rock*, Utah History Atlas, 2000.
Moore, Rebecca Estelle. *Children of the Trail*, Church of Jesus Christ of Latter-day Saints Archives.
Morgan, Martha. *A Trip Across the Plains, Journal*, Church of Jesus Christ of Latter-day Saints Archives, 1849.
MormonWiki. *Perpetual Emigration Fund*, http://www.mormonwiki.com.
Native American Nations. Collection of books and papers, www.Nanations.com.
Native American Languages, website: http://www.native-languages.org/

National Parks Service. *Mormon Pioneer Historic Research.*
  http://www.nps.gov/history
Nielsen, Jens. *Quotes Found in the book, "Hole in the Rock"* Utah History Atlas, 2000.
Osborn, David. *Reminiscences and journal*, 1860-1893, 23-25.
Palmer, Joel. *Personal Diary*, Mormon Pioneer Overland Travel, 1847–1868.
Parker, Donna Gene Smith. *Our Pioneer History*, Mike King custodian.
Putnam, Savannah. *Personal Diary*, Quoted in Walton Family Journals.
Richards, F.D. *1850 Voyage of The Ellen.* BYU Harold B. Lee Library
Roberts, Brigham Henry. *The Life of John Taylor*, George Q. Cannon and Sons, Co., 1892.
Rowley, Samuel. *Autobiography Quotes Found in the book, "Hole in the Rock"* Utah History Atlas, 2000.
Ship Master, *"Rules for Passengers"* Queen's Order in Council, October 6, 1849
Sonne, Conway B. *Saints on the Seas.* University of Utah Press, 2001.
Stanton, Bette Larsen. *Tom Roach Cowboy and Fast Gun*, article.
Swensen, Jason N. *Shipwreck Serves as Testament of Resiliency of LDS Pioneers*, Deseret News Archives, March 19, 1997.
Tanner, Faun McConkie. *The Far Country: A Regional History of Moab and La Sal, Utah*, Olympus Publishing Company, 1976.
Tanner, Rebecca Estela Moore, *Journal*, LDS History Library
The Bible. King James Version.
The First 100 Years in Woodruff, Stuart (out of print)
Turner, A. *Rules for Passengers*, TheShipsList.com Queens Order in Council, October 6, 1849.
Utah War. *The Utah War*, http://www.britannica.com, www.utah.gov, www.encyclopedia.com, www.media.utah.edu, www.wilkipedia.com.
Wagon Train Rules of 1853
Walton, Charles E. Sr. *Personal Journal*, Mike King custodian.
Walton, Charles E. Jr. *Personal Journal*, Mike King custodian.
Walton, Pearl C. *Personally Compiled Walton Family History*, Mike King custodian.
Wilson, Mark. The Encyclopedia of Chicago, Schuttler, http://www.encyclopedia.chicagohistory.org.
Young, Brigham. *Journal of Discourses*, F.D. and S.W. Richards, 1854.

    Mike King has worked in the law enforcement field for over 40 years. He received a BA and an MA in Criminal Justice and began his career as a police officer in northern Utah. He became an investigator in the Weber County Attorney's Office and subsequently in the Utah Attorney General's Office where he also served as Chief of Staff. He trained in criminal profiling under FBI Special Agent Gregory Cooper (ret.). He and Cooper were the investigators for the Discovery Channel's Emmy Award winning investigative documentary: Who Killed King Tut? He entered the private sector in 2004 and began working for Environmental Systems Research Institute (Esri) as the global director of emergency communications and fraud. Other books he has authored are: *Deceived, An Investigative Memoir of the Zion Society Cult, Who Killed King Tut, Predators: Who They Are and How to Stop Them and Profilers.* He and his wife, Bonnie, are the parents of three children and they have four grandchildren.

To inquire about booking Mike King for a speaking engagement, please contact ProfilingEvil.com
An audio and digital edition of this book is also available.
Profiling Evil, LLC

www.ingramcontent.com/pod-product-compliance
Lightning Source LLC
Chambersburg PA
CBHW042322090526
44585CB00025BA/2800